FRONTIERS OF SCIENCE

This intriguing series encompasses exciting trends and discoveries in areas of human exploration and progress: astronomy, anthropology, biology, physics, geology, medicine, health, genetics, and evolution. Sometimes controversial, these timely volumes present stimulating new points of view about our universe . . . and ourselves. Among the titles:

On Civilized Stars:
The Search for Intelligent Life in Outer Space
Joseph F. Baugher

Toward a New Brain:
Evolution and the Human Mind
Stuart Litvak and A. Wayne Senzee

The Human Body and Why It Works
Raymond L. Powis

Ancestral Voices:
Language and the Evolution of Human Consciousness
Curtis G. Smith

*Language and the Evolution of
Human Consciousness*

Ancestral
Voices

Curtis G. Smith

Illustrations by
Katherine A. Dorfman

A SPECTRUM BOOK

Prentice-Hall, Inc., Englewood Cliffs, New Jersey 07632

Library of Congress Cataloging in Publication Data

Smith, Curtis G.
   Ancestral voices.

   (Frontiers of science series)
   "A Spectrum Book."
   Bibliography: p.
   Includes index.
   1. Genetic psychology.   2. Consciousness.
3. Psycholinguistics.   4. Brain.   5. Human
information processing.   I. Title.   II. Series.
BF701.S48 1985   155.7   84-18231
ISBN 0-13-036187-9
ISBN 0-13-036179-8 (pbk.)

This book is available at a special discount when
ordered in bulk quantities. Contact Prentice-Hall, Inc.,
General Publishing Division, Special Sales,
Englewood Cliffs, N.J. 07632.

The quotation from "In the Fashion" by A. A. Milne from his book *When We Were Very
Young,* copyright 1924 by E. P. Dutton and Co., Inc., renewed 1952
by A. A. Milne, is reprinted by permission of E. P. Dutton, Inc., and
Methuen Children's Books. *(Continued on page 178.)*

Editorial/production supervision
and book design by Eric Newman
Chapter openings and title page by Alice R. Mauro
Cover design by Hal Siegel
Cover illustration by Richard Williams
Manufacturing buyer: Frank Grieco

ISBN 0-13-036187-9

ISBN 0-13-036179-8 {PBK.}

PRENTICE-HALL INTERNATIONAL, INC., *London*
PRENTICE-HALL OF AUSTRALIA PTY. LIMITED, *Sydney*
PRENTICE-HALL CANADA INC., *Toronto*
PRENTICE-HALL HISPANOAMERICANA, S.A., *Mexico*
PRENTICE-HALL OF INDIA PRIVATE LIMITED, *New Delhi*
PRENTICE-HALL OF JAPAN, INC., *Tokyo*
PRENTICE-HALL OF SOUTHEAST ASIA PTE. LTD., *Singapore*
WHITEHALL BOOKS LIMITED, *Wellington, New Zealand*
EDITORA PRENTICE-HALL DO BRASIL LTDA., *Rio de Janeiro*

*This book is dedicated to Timothy Griffin Collett,
whose fluent babbling during its preparation
gave joyous testimony to the powerful drive
toward language that is the birthright
of every human child.*

Contents

Foreword

This book addresses the way in which the human brain processes information. It is timely, for the neurosciences have made prodigious advances in recent years, and this new knowledge connects with parallel advances in the processing of information by machines.

Since the beginnings of electronic information processing systems four decades ago, scientists and engineers have tried to develop machines that would emulate human intelligence. While computers perform complex calculations and repetitive tasks with astonishing speed and accuracy, only modest progress has been made in causing machines to perform tasks that would be described as intelligent if they were done by humans; we are barely at the threshold of the field of artificial intelligence.

Much of the difficulty of developing machines that perform higher-order tasks inheres in our lack of understanding of the detailed manner in which the human brain functions. This book explores recent advances in the understanding of brain function, including issues related to vision, memory, and the pervasive use of a symbolic code that makes language possible. Not only do these important questions underlie our efforts to understand brain function, they also contribute greatly to our ability to design machines that may come closer to the ambitious goals of artificial intelligence. For example, joint contributions of psychologists, neurobiologists, and computer scientists to unraveling the problems implicit in human vision shed much light on parallel processing techniques applicable to computers and move us closer to the objective of computer vision.

While this book is entirely contemporary in its perspective, it is rooted in a period twenty to thirty years ago when work done at M.I.T. in the Research Laboratory of Electronics was changing our understanding of the way in which information is represented and processed in both biological and machine systems. This work, thoroughly interdisciplinary in character, gave birth to the modern science of linguistics. It is mirrored today in studies of cognition, brain science, and artificial intelligence that span several departments and laboratories, even as it is reflected in Professor Smith's early associations and work in the neurosciences.

PAUL E. GRAY
*president, Massachusetts
Institute of Technology*

Preface

Recent discoveries in the rich fossil beds of Africa have filled some of the gaps in the record of human evolution, just at the time that ferment in evolutionary theory has revolutionized much of our thinking about human origins. At the same time, a revolution of a different kind has taken place in our understanding of how the mind works. Sparked by the explosive increase in our understanding of information processing, neuroscience has made more progress in the last few years than in the preceding century, particularly in the study of the higher functions, such as language and consciousness. This book attempts to bring together the current thinking in the fields of anthropology, linguistics, evolution, and the neurosciences as it applies to the mystery of human origins. It focuses on one all-important step in our evolutionary history—the emergence of consciousness. That step carried us over the threshold from beast to human. When did it happen? How long did it take? What brought it about? The answers to these questions will bring us to a deeper understanding of the nature of language and of its inseparable relationship to human consciousness. In the final chapter we explore the question of the uniqueness of language, and how much the human brain differs from those of other animals.

Other topics, intimately related to the subject matter of this book, are not directly addressed but are implicit in much of the discussion. Among these are questions about the definition and measurement of human intelligence, and the degree to which it depends on innate endowment, as opposed to training and acculturation. The perennial debate over the relative importance of heredity and environment has sparked social and educational experiments that have often been as disastrous as they were inconclusive. Readers who believe in the primacy of nature over nurture should find satisfaction in the assertion that biological mechanisms created a linguistic capability before any human language was invented, and that language and consciousness are natural evolutionary consequences of certain purely neurological developments. Readers who believe that intelligence is a product of civilization and training will also find support for their convictions. Cultural evolution is presented as such a powerful agency in hominid development that biological evolution has, for all practical purposes, become irrelevant for humans ever since language and consciousness emerged.

The final message of the book should bring some satisfaction to readers on both sides of the nature/nurture debate. The potential of both the biological and the cultural wellsprings of our intellectual development has scarcely begun to be realized. The efficiency of our mental processes is still far from optimal: The expansion of the information processing capacity of our brains by a thousandfold could be managed without any increase in physical size or number of neurons.

The ideas in this book have been germinating for a number of years, and it is impossible to acknowledge all of the friends, students, and colleagues who have contributed by their interest, criticism, and discussion. Members of the Department of Electrical Engineering at the Massachusetts Institute of Technology were particularly influential at the early stages of my interest in this subject. That department was the unquestioned leader in the early research and development of theories in both computer and neural processes. I am especially grateful to Paul Gray, now the president of M.I.T., who was chairman of the Electrical Engineering Department during those wonderful years when it seemed that most of the great names in the emerging fields of cybernetics and brain science were gathered there. It is not merely punning to say that the atmosphere was electric. Paul nurtured a very heterogeneous group of individuals in their various pursuits, and his department encouraged an unusually wide range of inquiry. He has graciously contributed a foreword to this book.

The final research and writing of the manuscript were aided by a Mellon Grant, which made it possible to finish the work

PREFACE

within a single sabbatical leave. I am very grateful to the staff of the British Library, the Musée de l'Homme in Paris, the Rheinisches Landesmuseum in Bonn, and the Department of Physical Anthropology of Cambridge University for their cooperation. Those whom I must particularly mention for their help, influence, and expertise happen to be very close friends. Isabelle Sprague not only provided answers to specific questions but in the years of our association in the Biology Department of Mount Holyoke College has labored to teach me zoology. Although I stubbornly remain a neurophysiologist, she has greatly improved the breadth of my biological vision. Stan Rachootin, who only recently joined our department, has served as a source of information and has stimulated my thinking in many areas of evolutionary theory. Stephen and Peggy Davol, with whom I discussed much of this material, preceded me as Mellon Scholars, exploring the motor and intellectual capabilities of prehistoric man through a study of his tools and other artifacts. They were immensely helpful in directing me to certain fossil collections and to experts in archeology and anthropology. Steve's tragic and unexpected death interrupted their work and left an unfillable void in the lives of all of his colleagues. Peggy has generously shared their finds; this manuscript has benefited from her knowledge and insight.

My final acknowledgement is to my wife, Elaine. Many authors find it appropriate to mention their debt to their wives and families for the support and comfort tendered during the writing of a book. I have been abundantly supplied with support and comfort, but my gratitude for such matters can be expressed less publicly. It is my good fortune to be married to an editor of considerable skill and experience, who provided invaluable help and scholarly advice at every stage of this undertaking. Whatever grace and elegance it may have are tributes to her skill. Its shortcomings are mine.

CURTIS G. SMITH (Ph.D., University of Chicago) is a professor of biological sciences at Mount Holyoke College in Massachusetts.

Introduction

Standing in the snow, a few kilometers east of Düsseldorf, I looked up a narrow valley. The shadows of the February afternoon made the snow look blue. Steep sides of the wooded valley curved with the meanders of the little stream. A few hundred feet from where I stood rose a huge vine-covered rock: a slab of limestone that had once been a part of the steep valley wall. Quarriers had removed most of the surrounding rock a hundred years ago, but this piece had been spared. High on the face was a stone plaque with the legend:

Zur Erinnerung
an die Entdeckung
des
Neanderthal
Menschen
Prof. Dr. G. Fuhlrott
Elberfeld
im Sommer 1856*

How incredible that this special place had been preserved unspoiled in the midst of industrial Germany! Three hun-

*"In memory of the discovery of Neanderthal Man by Prof. Dr. G. Fuhlrott, Elberfeld, in the summer of 1856."

dred years ago the poet and composer Johann Neumann (more familiar by the Greek form of his name, Neander) grew so fond of its beauty that after his untimely death the local people began to call it "Neander's valley" (*Neander Thal* in the old German spelling). Two hundred years later, in a cave that "Neander" had picnicked in, the quarry men found the bones of what we now call Neanderthal man.

In his publication of the find Professor Fuhlrott referred to the cave as Feldhofer grotto, and the valley as Düsselthal. It was only when a full taxonomic description of the skeleton was made a decade later that the local name for this valley was used, and our most immediate ancestor became known as *Homo neanderthalensis*.

And here I stood, steeped in the study of fossil man, in a spot where archeological history was made. In the quiet and loneliness of this place it was easy to imagine a troop of Neanderthals trudging down the snow-covered path beside the stream. They would be used to the cold, but perhaps a warm fire awaited them in the cave that was a few minutes' walk from where I watched. One of them, a middle-aged man with a twisted arm, was soon to die, but his bones were destined to achieve a kind of immortality.

Were these heavy-browed, chinless creatures human? Recent amendments to primate taxonomy have placed them in a separate subspecies from their fully human successors. *Homo sapiens neanderthalensis* is what we now call them, while Cro-Magnon man and all living humans are *Homo sapiens sapiens*. The final crucial evolutionary jump that crossed the threshold from a two-legged, tool-using, large-brained beast to a self-conscious, artistic, culture-dominated human being must have taken place within the Neanderthal species, but when it did, he was no longer the "classical Neanderthal" of this cave, but the transitional form that became the new subspecies we know as Cro-Magnon.

Archeology was still primitive in 1856, and there were no tools or animal bones found with the skeleton to help Professor Fuhlrott's investigations, so to this day we are unable to date the fossil with confidence. My guess is that this crippled old man of my imagination was still not fully human. Smarter than any chimpanzee, master of fire, and possessor of a few crude skills for chipping flints, he did not yet have the unique gift of language. Language would have raised him from the limitations of his direct sensory experience, enabling him to create for himself a world of consciousness, reverie, imagination, and experimentation. The story of how language and consciousness developed in this not-quite-human ancestor will be unfolded in this book.

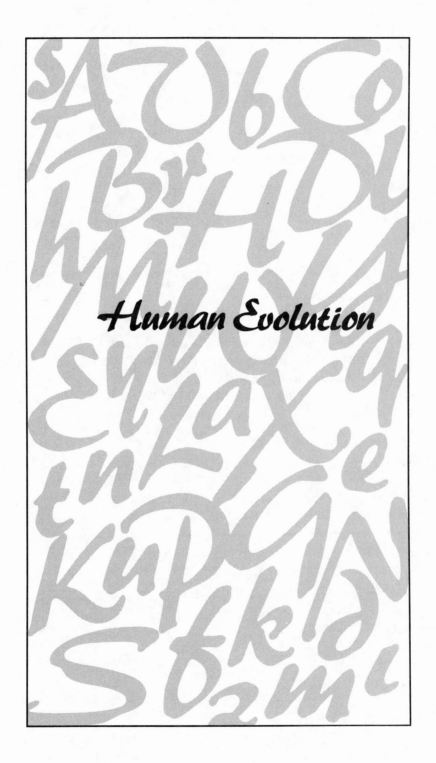

Human Evolution

A lion has a tail and a very fine tail
And so has an elephant, and so has a whale,
And so has a crocodile, and so has a quail—
They've all got tails but me.

A. A. MILNE[1]

THE MOST CRUCIAL EVENT in human evolution was the final breakthrough into consciousness, for it is consciousness that distinguishes humans from the beasts. Any living thing that has a brain may have some degree of consciousness, but only humans have a stream of internal dialogue between the senses, reporting on the outside world, and the person, the *self*, the *me*. Self-awareness and the capacity to dream, imagine, remember, and create are the hallmarks of humanity, and all are components of what we call human consciousness. How did such capabilities arise out of the lesser qualities of sensory awareness and instinctive responses? When, in the history of human evolution, did consciousness emerge? This book provides tentative answers to these questions, based on recent discoveries and speculations of anthropologists, psychologists, and neuroscientists. The answers have to be tentative. Consciousness is one of the least accessible evolutionary characteristics to trace. It does not leave fossils. We can deduce the quality of consciousness in early man only by a study of his artifacts, and by extrapolation from comparative studies of living animals.

The story of human evolution is complex, controversial, and fragmentary. It is complex because it involves all parts of the body. We differ from other vertebrates in many ways besides the development of a specialized brain with the capacity for consciousness. Among other things, human evolution led to the development of erect, bipedal locomotion, the acquisition of the hand with an opposable thumb, the decrease of body fur, and the loss of that most useful appendage, the tail.

Controversies about human evolution come about partly from the special biases we have about our own past, plus the weight of religious and cultural traditions concerning our origins. Such controversies are hard to settle because firm evidence for much of the evolutionary history of our species is lacking, largely because of the fragmentary nature of the fossil record. There is something mysterious about the paucity of human fossils. Possibly early hominids disposed of their dead in ways that did not favor the preservation of the bones. Certainly many more stone tools and artifacts than human bones have been found in the major sites of excavation. Richard Leakey has commented that all of the known fossils of our ancestors and their close relatives dated between six million and fifteen million years ago could be kept in a single shoebox. And to display all of the fossils older than one million years would require only a couple of good-sized tables. Faced with the meagerness of the evidence, the anthropologist finds it hard to determine whether a certain difference in form is a significant evolutionary development or simply a random variation within members of the same species. Even trying to determine the sex of the individual whose fragmentary skeleton is being examined can lead to confusion. Humans, as well as other animals, have anatomical differences between the sexes that are not limited to the primary sex organs. Although we do not have such extremes of sexual differentiation as, say, the antlers of deer, the bones of a woman are generally smaller and more delicate in their modeling than those of a man. These differences can confuse the paleontologist trying to determine the degree of robustness of a fossil hominid from a single bone of unknown gender.

Before focusing on the critical segment of the long history of human evolution that witnessed the breakthrough into consciousness, it is appropriate to sketch the larger context of evolutionary developments that led to that last jump into full humanity.

In the 600-million-year history of the animal kingdom the hominids are relative latecomers. The earliest primates appeared about 70 million years ago, probably as arboreal insect-eaters. The order Primata evolved into two suborders, the Anthropoidea and the Prosimii. The anthropoids later diverged into several families that encompass all of the present apes and monkeys. One of these, the superfamily Hominoidea, gave rise to three families, the Hylobatidae (gibbons), the Pongidae (gorillas, orangutans, and chimpanzees), and the Hominidae. This last division took place sometime between 15 and 20 million years ago, in the Miocene epoch, according to geological evidence. Molecular similarities between human and ape hemoglobins and other DNA and protein molecules suggest a more recent divergence between man and the great apes. There is some disagreement about the relationships within the pongids, as well as between the pongid and hominid families based on newer fossil finds. If we take tool making and the use of fire as a characteristic of the hominids and not of the pongids, then the earliest occurrence of worked stone implements provides a minimum date for the evolutionary emergence of the non-ape hominoid. That date is presently estimated at about two-and-a-half million years ago, which agrees fairly well with the molecular evidence for the final divergence between man and the gorilla.

Much of the fossil evidence for the earliest hominid and ape precursors comes from rich deposits in the Fayum region of the Nile delta. A crucial period of from one to five million years ago, when the genus *Homo* began to emerge, has been illuminated by finds from the Olduvai Gorge, Lake Turkana, and a few other sites in Ethiopia and South Africa. The total of all these discoveries is still insufficient to give a very confident outline of human evolution.

Despite the multitude of new finds and the explosive increase in information about our human ancestors, the classification of all of the hominid fossils remains a confusing and controversial topic. The system of taxonomy does not make the situation any easier. It was invented by Carl Linne one hundred years before Darwin's theory of evolution made it apparent that species are not immutable (see Figure 1). In the Linnean system of taxonomy, the line of demarcation between members of two different species is determined by a number of biological criteria. It is very hard to determine the proper classification in an evolving sequence, especially when looking at a single individual, perhaps represented by only a few fragments of fossil bone.

Historically the first discovery of a fossil man was that of the Neanderthal cave skeleton in 1856 (Figure 2). Not until fifty years later did other finds give sufficient evidence to establish that Neanderthal man was indeed a taxonomic entity (Figure 3). The original designation made Neanderthals and modern man separate species. More recent practice is to include both in the same species, *Homo sapiens*, but as two subspecies—*Homo sapiens neanderthalensis* and *Homo sapiens sapiens*.

Other hominid species have not received as satisfactory a taxonomic placement. There is no other extinct hominid for which we have recovered anything approaching the abundance of individual specimens as we have of Neanderthal. When there is a large evolutionary gap between two separate finds it is difficult to decide species boundaries. One version of our probable evolutionary history is shown in Figure 4. Not all authorities would agree with all parts of this diagram. As new discoveries are made, a more confident assignment of the existing specimens will probably emerge.

If we start with the earliest true hominids we must go back about three million years, to the divergence between the families Pongidae and Hominidae. This is before the beginning of the Pleistocene period. An extinct genus of apes called *Ramapithecus* is perhaps the first named specimen of this line. The genus gets its name from the Indian mythical hero Rama (*pithecus* means ape). The first fossil was found in India in 1932 by Edward Lewis (Figure 5). Other ramapithecine finds have been made in Africa by Louis Leakey, and in

Figure 1. Carl Linne, inventor of modern taxonomy, assumed that each species had been created separately. Nevertheless, he developed an elaborate system of relationships among organisms based largely on their form and structure that remains remarkably valid as an expression of genuine evolutionary bonds. It was somewhat daring in the early eighteenth century to place human beings in a taxonomic relationship with apes and to recognize our remoter relationship with other mammals and then with all vertebrates, but Linnaeus (the Latinized form of his name, under which he published his scientific works) did not mean to imply any more about the relationship among animals in a common genus or order than he did about rocks, which he also included in his grand taxonomic scheme. (Oil painting of Linne as a bridegroom.)

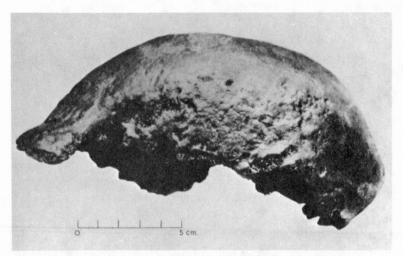

Figure 2. The skull of the first Neanderthal fossil, discovered in Feldhofer grotto in 1856. The skeleton was nearly complete when found, but as its significance was not appreciated for some years, much of it has been lost. (Photographed in the Rheinisches Landesmuseum, Bonn.)

Greece, Turkey, Hungary, and Pakistan. This creature was much more ape-like than human, but it may have been the ancestor of another extinct genus, *Australopithecus*. The australopithecines are assigned ancestral status for modern man with more confidence than *Ramapithecus*, but many problems remain unsolved. No other good candidate is known for the immediate predecessor of genus *Homo*. Australopithecine fossils are fairly widespread in Africa, and the picture is complicated by the fact that there are two types, a robust and a gracile strain. It seems likely that the smaller, lighter-framed form is the more primitive. The first discovery from this group was made in 1924 by a limestone quarryman, M. de Bruyn, in a cave about six miles from the Taung railway station, near Kimberley. It was the skull of a juvenile with the facial region and lower jaw fairly intact, but missing the vault of the cranium (Figure 6). However, there is a remarkably complete endocast of the interior of the original skull, which gives a very good idea of the external morphology of the brain. When R. A. Dart published the discovery the following year, he named it *Australopithecus africanus*.

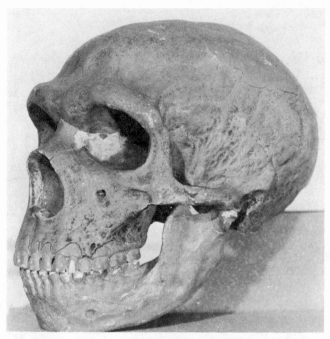

Figure 3. The second major Neanderthal find was made in
a small cave called La Chapelle-aux-Saints a few miles
south of Tulle in southern France, August 3, 1908. The
excavation was made with unusual thoroughness and care,
and numerous flints of typical late Mousterian type were
found, along with bones of the woolly rhinoceros and other
extinct mammals. The nearly complete skeleton was used
by M. Boule as a "type specimen" in establishing the
taxonomic category *Homo neanderthalensis* (since replaced
by the current placement as a sub-species of *Homo
sapiens*). Boule was misled in his reconstruction of Neanderthal
man from this skeleton. The bones are distorted by
osteoarthritis, which led him to picture a stooped,
bent-kneed posture and slouching gait. Although we now
know that Neanderthal walked erect, this early mistake is
immortalized in the popular and cartoon version of
"cavemen." (Photographed in the Musée de l'Homme,
Paris.)

Assigning a new genus name to a single individual is always
risky, especially when the fossil is from an immature animal.
Dart ably defended his taxonomic boldness, largely on the
basis of the human characteristics of the teeth; and later

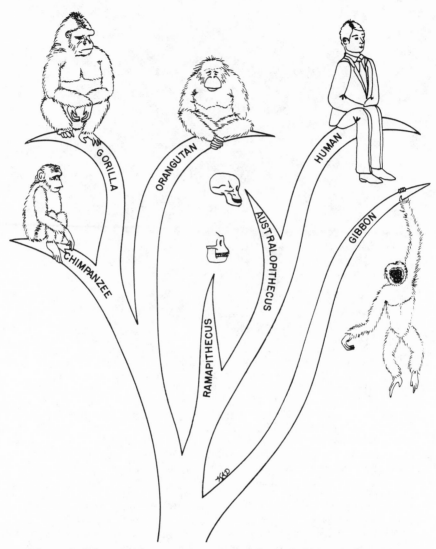

Figure 4. Diagram of a current version of the probable evolutionary relationships among the hominids and the great apes. Only a few of the many extinct lines of hominids are shown.

finds, mainly from South Africa, have vindicated his opinion. The Taung baby was a member of the gracile branch of the australopithecines. Further development apparently led to a larger and more specialized robust form, but the later species is probably not on the direct line of human evolution.

Figure 5. Ramapithecus. This early ape may have
been the first known representative of the line that
diverged from the pongids and became the hominid
branch of the primates.

Additional problems surround the placement of the
australopithecines in our ancestry. The genus *Homo*, which
presumably emerged from the genus *Australopithecus*,
seems to have already appeared in Java before the time of
some of the Transvaal remains, which makes it more likely
that the African forms were collateral descendants of a common ancestor who died out before the end of the Pleistocene.
Whatever the actual relationships may be, the australopithecine fossils are the main evidence we have for the last stages
of evolution before the emergence of the genus *Homo*.

The recent discovery of "Lucy," the most complete
australopithecine skeleton yet found, has excited new interest in this period. One of the major lessons from this outstanding discovery is that a fully man-like erect posture and
striding gait were achieved before any spectacular development of the brain (see Figure 7).

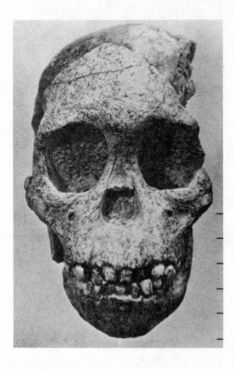

Figure 6. The Taung Baby. Found in November 1924, it was the first australopithecine fossil to be recognized in Africa. (Original in the University of the Witwatersrand, Johannesburg.)

When we trace the evolutionary sequence leading toward man, the taxonomic boundaries become more difficult to place as we get closer to our goal. The species is the only truly natural taxonomic category, for good biological criteria determine the distinctions between species. Higher taxa, such as genus and family, are more or less arbitrary inventions that make convenient partitions among what we believe to be genuine biological relationships. The transition into the genus *Homo* is especially difficult to date, partly because of disagreement over the precise definition of what should be the boundaries between genera, but also because of disagreement over what features are really uniquely characteristic of *man*. The discovery of Lucy showed us that the erect two-legged posture was already present before our genus evolved, so we look for a marked increase in brain size, development of the hand, and tool use as appropriate distinguishing characteristics. These features appeared between two and three million years ago, so we may assume that our genus evolved toward the end of that time span.

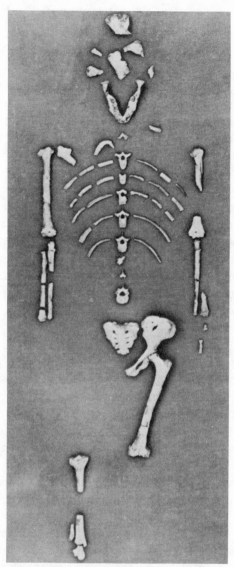

Figure 7. "Lucy," found in Ethiopia by
Donald Johanson in 1974, is the most
complete early australopithecine fossil yet
found. There is enough of the skeleton to
provide strong evidence for a fully erect
bipedal posture, but the brain is still very
small and ape-like. Whether or not this
exciting find is on our direct ancestral line,
it does cast light on the sequence of
bipedalism and brain enlargement.

The earliest fossil evidence for emergence of our own genus dates to 1891, when Eugene Dubois found a fossil skull in Central Java (Figure 8). The site was near the Lawu volcano, a few yards from the river Solo. A little farther upstream he found a femur that is assumed to come from the same individual. Study of the femur showed remarkable similarities to those of modern man and strongly implied an erect stance. At the time Dubois published his find in 1894, it was not clear how ancient the erect posture was in human evolution, so he assigned the name *Pithecanthropus erectus* (erect ape-man) to his discovery. The genus name has since been superseded, and we now designate Java man as a very early member of the genus *Homo*; but the species name, *erectus*, has been retained. So the name "erect man" is established for our most nearly human ancestors, even though the erect posture had already been achieved by considerably more primitive hominids.

Additional finds in Africa, largely by the Leakeys, have both reinforced and complicated the sequence suggested by the Java fossils. Louis Leakey proposed a transitional species, *Homo habilis*, represented by Olduvai Gorge finds dated to one and three-quarter million years ago. If this classification were accepted it would be difficult to know where to draw the line between it and *Homo erectus*. There are still too few fossils to make an unambiguous sequence for this critical period in human evolution. At present we do not know how many species there may have been within the genus *Homo*.

The evolution of our own species, *Homo sapiens*, is one of the hardest steps to pin down. The study of recent evolution is complicated by the glaciation that affected much of Europe during the critical period. Earlier fossils, already deeply embedded in the rocky crust of the earth, might escape the grinding and dislocating effects of the great sheets of ice, but more recent deposits were more likely to be destroyed unless they were protected in caves or preserved by other lucky accidents. Another problem is that as we look at more nearly contemporary materials our greater knowledge

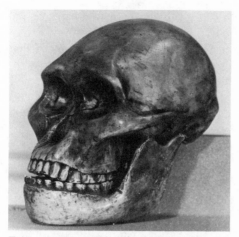

Figure 8. "Java Man," called *Pithecanthropus erectus* by its discoverer, Eugene Dubois, was found in 1891. Subsequent finds have revised the taxonomy of hominids, and this skull is now considered to be one of the very earliest representatives of our own genus. It is probably related to Peking Man. A similar fossil was found in 1937, about 40 miles east of the Dubois site. (Original in the Rijksuniversiteit te Utrecht, Netherlands.)

makes our judgment more critical. It is easy to tell that two fossils separated in time by many thousands of years of evolution belong to different species. When we get closer to our own time we have a more nearly continuous series, so the placing of a taxonomic boundary between closely related individuals becomes more difficult.

The uneasiness of some anthropologists is expressed by Jan Jelinek, who, in a Nobel Symposium on Early Man held in 1978, said,

> There is no good reason, anatomical or cultural, why we should separate middle pleistocene and upper pleistocene hominids into two separate species, namely, into *Homo erectus* and *Homo sapiens*.

There is only a fluent transition from the more archaic complex of traits in older finds to a more
progressive morphology, with the main change in
the degree of cerebralization bound up with social
and cultural developments.[2]

Jelinek forgets that, with rare exceptions, the course of evolution is *always* a matter of "fluent transitions." Like the
growth of a child, it seems imperceptible to the continuous
observer, but for a visiting uncle seeing only brief segments
of the process, each encounter elicits a surprised "How
much you have grown!" Only the incompleteness of our fossil record makes it possible to set up distinct steps in the sequence. Perhaps the more recent evolutionary changes are
simply too well documented to permit us to draw an arbitrary line between species.

Homo erectus did evolve, whether fluently or by
abrupt changes, into *Homo sapiens*, and the first representatives of our own species to tread the earth were the Neanderthals. By far the greatest number of Neanderthal fossils are
from the European region, but that does not imply that the
first true men were evolved in Europe. Neanderthal and Ne-
anderthal-like bones have turned up in Africa, the Far East,
and the Eastern Mediterranean. European specimens pre-
dominate because the triangular region of southern France,
between the Atlantic Ocean, the Alps, and the Pyrenees,
happened to be an exceptionally rich and fruitful region during the last glacial epoch, and it must have supported an unusually large population of Neanderthal and, later, Cro-
Magnon people. The same region has an abundance of
limestone caves, and the cave environment is especially
likely to result in the preservation of fossil remains. If we
were to subtract those cave finds from the total of known
Neanderthal relics, we would not find Europe a particularly
rich hunting ground.

We regard Neanderthal as a single subspecies, but in
the long span of their existence Neanderthals showed a

marked evolutionary development. Therefore the first members of that race differed considerably from the last. The earliest known neanderthaloid fossils are difficult to place securely, as they are transitional from *erectus* to *sapiens*. This is particularly hard with the Swanscombe skull (see Figure 9), as it does not include the facial portions, and so one cannot observe whether it has the characteristic Neanderthal brow ridges.

In the Steinheim skull, found near Stuttgart in 1933, two years before the first of the Swanscombe finds, much more of the facial structure has been preserved (Figure 10). The heavy brow ridges and broad nasal opening give it ob-

Figure 9. The Swanscombe skull, found in three separate fragments on three separate occasions over a period of twenty years. A. T. Marston found the occipital bone on June 29, 1935. A year later, at the same site, he found the left parietal, which fits perfectly into the sutures of the other bone. Twenty years later, on July 30, 1955, the other parietal was found. All three bones fit together, as illustrated. (From the British Museum, London.)

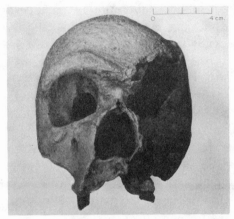

Figure 10. The Steinheim skull was found in a river gravel deposit near Stuttgart, July 24, 1933, two years before the first of the Swanscombe finds. It is more complete than the Swanscombe fossil but appears to be closely related, and the facial portions show obvious similarities to Neanderthal. (From the Staatliches Museum fur Naturkunde, Stuttgart.)

vious similarities to the Neanderthal skulls, but it, too, is very early, with primitive features that also suggest a transitional stage between *erectus* and *sapiens*.

There are noticeable differences in the Neanderthal skulls found in different parts of the world, just as there are differences in the skulls of modern Chinese, Scandinavians, black Africans, and other populations. The European Neanderthal is called the "classical Neanderthal," which may simply reflect a bias induced by the great preponderance of European fossils.

The other end of the Neanderthal era provides a different kind of problem. Again, the fossil record is tantalizingly incomplete, but the major difficulty is not in finding a place to draw the taxonomic line between one species and the one that succeeded it. Instead, the line is *too* clear. In European sites, at least, the Neanderthal line ends abruptly, to be replaced by Cro-Magnon, and there is no clear record of transitional changes in either the fossils or in the cultural artifacts. Cro-Magnon was the name given to the first fossils of our own subspecies, *Homo sapiens sapiens* (Figure 11). The discovery was accidental, during the excavation of a limestone cliff for a railroad cutting, at Cro-Magnon, in the Dordogne region of France. Five adult skeletons plus some fragmentary infant bones were found, along with many Aurignacian flints and the bones of a number of extinct mammals. From the time of their original publication in 1868, the remains were recognized as being of our own species, and not Neanderthal. Cro-Magnon continues to be regarded almost as a type specimen for all fossils of *Homo sa-*

Figure 11. The Cro-Magnon "Old Man," found with four other adult skeletons and some infant and fetal remains in 1868. This skull was the best preserved of the group and has served as the archetype for Cro-Magnon morphology. Although contemporary with some Neanderthal fossils, this skull shows the complete loss of the heavy brow ridges and massive nasal bones of the Neanderthals and has a distinct chin exactly like our own. (Photographed in the Musée de l'Homme, Paris.)

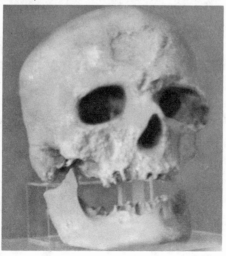

piens sapiens, although technically this is probably an unnecessary formality for our own species. Except for the physical anthropologist, the study of the skeletons of our immediate predecessors becomes less important than observation of artifacts; and, indeed, the usual practice in most discussions is to classify discoveries of our more recent ancestors by their cultural affinities, rather than by skeletal types. As with Neanderthal, and as with modern man, the Cro-Magnon people from different regions show racial differences. The variations among the known fossils do not indicate continued physical evolutionary progress within the last 50,000 years. Cro-Magnon, insofar as his biological form can be known, was fully modern, and if one of them were to walk among us today he would not be recognized as unusual.

Abundant evidence indicates that, in Europe at least, Cro-Magnon and Neanderthal overlapped in time. That fact presents difficulties. The "Neanderthal problem" is created by the evolutionist dogma that a population cannot be both ancestral and sympatric to another population; that is, new species cannot evolve from old as long as they are interbreeding, because the common gene pool shared by a group of interbreeding individuals is what defines a species. Members of the same species who are living in the same place at the same time (sympatric) are unlikely to remain in reproductive isolation for long enough periods to develop distinctive gene pools. Thus if Neanderthal is indeed the ancestor of modern man (and there is no other candidate), Cro-Magnon must have descended from an isolated branch of the Neanderthal population and then have reinvaded the European homeland of the "classical" Neanderthals after the evolutionary differences were firmly established. Whether these two subspecies could interbreed, as imagined in recent popular novels, is impossible to say. In any event, Neanderthal became extinct within a very short time after the appearance of Cro-Magnon. Most prehistorians assume that Cro-Magnon, with his superior culture and technology, simply wiped out his closest rival for the riches of Europe. The extinction would not be any more remarkable than more recent cases such as the fate of the Patagonians. A number of human populations have virtually disappeared after their homelands were invaded by bearers of a different culture.

A possible locale for the final evolutionary shift from Neanderthal to Cro-Magnon is the Eastern Mediterranean region. Some of the fossils found in the caves of Mount Carmel, a few miles south of Haifa, may be transitional. Other recent finds give additional support to a Near Eastern locale for this last step in the long history of human evolution.

This brief survey of the biological evolution of man has evaded the real subject of our concern, the origin of consciousness. Although consciousness itself does not leave fossils, evidence for the development of man's mental abilities can be found in his activities, some of which do leave permanent records for the archeologist to uncover. And so, to unfold the story of the evolution of consciousness we must look again at the chronology of the last million years of human evolution, but this time we will focus on the artifacts found in the living sites of early man, rather than at the changes in his body.

The sum of the activities that characterize a group of humans is called a culture. The culture of our extinct forebears can be but dimly perceived from the fragmentary relics of stone tools, an occasional hearth, or the site of the butchering of a large animal. From these small clues we can attempt to reconstruct the quality of mentality expressed by the activities, and we find that human culture, like the human body, has shown an evolutionary development from the simple and primitive toward the specialized and complex.

There is a growing tendency to regard all of evolution, not just human evolution, as an accumulation of usable *information*. Emphasis on information, rather than mere changes in form and function, has brought new insights to the study of evolution. At a fairly simplistic level it is obvious that an undifferentiated "primitive" organism is less complicated than a specialized multicellular organism largely because it "contains" less information. One way in which information increases is by the addition of more genetic material, which carries, encoded in the nucleic acid molecules, the directions for assembling a duplicate of the whole organism. It literally takes a longer code message to make a squirrel than to make a bacterial cell. This is not to argue that evolution should be judged entirely on the basis of genetic complexity, but it is true that a greater and greater amount of genetic information tends to accumulate as evolution proceeds. Thus one way of measuring biological success might be by asking how much information is available to the organism to help it succeed in the struggle to survive and to reproduce.

Another kind of information valuable for survival is that stored in the nervous system as memory. This neurological information—where the nest is, which way to go for water, how to outwit a predator—is acquired during the lifetime of the individual. Ordinarily it does not last longer than the individual lifespan, and each animal has to acquire its own store. It is difficult to make a meaningful comparison between these two kinds of information. Genetic information provides the structure, the physical capabilities, and much of the behavior of animals. Neurological information gives a more specific adaptation to the immediate needs of the individual. Of the two, genetic information seems more important than neurological information in terms of survival and evolutionary significance.

A third kind of information is available to animals. It is not stored in the genes, nor in the neural circuitry, but in the environment itself. We might call this cultural information. When animals actively modify the physical world in such a way as to leave a "message," the information impressed on the environment can be read and used to advantage. A deer path leading to a water hole is a simple example. A beehive is a more complex example: The honeycomb provides cues that organize the behavior of the bees to their benefit. Much of this "cultural information" is fairly ephemeral, and there are not many cases where its accumulation markedly affects the survival prospects of a species—except in humans. Perhaps the most important characteristic that distinguishes humans from all other organisms is that we are cultural animals, and our evolution in the last 50,000 years has been overwhelmingly dominated by the accumulation of cultural information, rather than genetic or even neurological information. Culture has achieved this leading role because cultural information can accumulate at a much faster rate than any other kind. Genetic changes are very slow. Neurological information is limited by the capacity of each individual, and in general it is not passed on, except insofar as it is transformed into cultural information. Not only is cultural information cumulative, but the process is largely self-generating, so that the rate of accumulation is ever accelerating. Tools are a good example of cultural information, and they illustrate the catalytic action that makes the increase of cultural information so rapid. A tool, persisting long after its creator has perished, serves both as a useful asset in itself and also as a store of information as to how more tools may be made. Thus it is self-reproducing. Furthermore, good tools may make it possible to invent even better tools, so the accumulation of cultural objects is an accelerating process. A stone scraper may be used to make a wooden hammer, which in turn can be used for the production of better stone implements. Particular cultural acquisitions had such immediate significance that they became milestones, or evolutionary jumps in our development. Fire, the needle, pottery, the wheel—one can recite a litany of cultural developments that drastically and irreversibly changed the history of mankind and that have molded the earth itself to a new environment, more friendly to human needs. Recognition of the catastrophic consequences of unwise environmental "molding" should not blind us to the fact that mankind could not survive at all without actively controlling his material resources. What is needed today is more control, not less. We have long since passed the point where we could rely on natural processes to dispose of our wastes, restore our fields and forests, and replenish the animal and plant populations we have decimated.

Human evolution has been characterized by all three classes of information—genetic, neurological, and cultural. It is tempting to rank the classes, since the perennial questions about the relative importance of innate and acquired characteristics in human development are obviously related to the role of genetic *versus* cultural evolution in shaping mankind. Genetic information is slow to change, conservative, and while it is the most fundamental element in the evolution of all organisms, it has become less important for humans since cultural evolution has become the dominant factor. Neurological information allows the individual to adapt very rapidly to new circumstances and is capable of very large jumps, creating novel and unexpected solutions to problems that innate mechanisms would be unable to cope with. Neurological information is the progenitor of cultural information. An idea about certain esoteric properties of semiconductors, existing as neurological information in the mind of one person, may become translated to a culture where every beach and sidewalk is filled with music from transistor radios. Culture permits the preservation and accumulation of the otherwise transitory neurological information. Information expressed as culture has both the persistence of the genetic changes and the volatility and capability for unexpected leaps that are found in neurological mechanisms, plus the important feature that it becomes self-generating and therefore tends to accumulate at an ever faster pace.

Culture is the defining characteristic of humanity. The material culture left by our prehistoric predecessors provides the best evidence we have of their evolutionary development. The few "pebble tools" of *Homo habilis*, which were quickly struck, carried at most a few miles, and casually discarded after use, betray a subhuman status for that species. Their culture was static, rudimentary, and far from dominating their development. They lived on what they found, moving on when things ran out, rather than molding and shaping the environment to suit their needs. Whatever shelters they may have built were, like the nests of birds or of chimpanzees, simply shelters, without plumbing, ornamentation, or ritual. They may have been successful, clever, and well adapted to their world, but they were not yet human. They had not been swept up in the accelerating rush of progress fueled by the positive feedback of culture.

To trace the evolution of man, then, requires that we stop looking at the fossil record of his genetically controlled changes at the point where genetic evolution ceased to be the governing factor in his progress. Ever since that time, which is within the last 100,000 years, cultural evolution has been the driving force, and we should look at his tools, art, and social institutions rather than at his bones to learn how we came to be.

It is unlikely that cultural dominance came suddenly. Fire, for example, was evidently a part of the culture of pre-humans for at least a million years. Even the few poor tools of the Oldowan culture (named by Leakey, from the Olduvai Gorge) showed a stability and uniformity that argues for a strong cultural tradition. As we come closer to the evolution of modern man, the Acheulian culture, which supplanted the Oldowan, was characterized by a hand axe, a vast improvement over the crude pebble tools that preceded it. The Acheulian hand axe technology evidently spread to all parts of Africa and was carried into a large part of Europe and Asia. Once a major technological improvement was made, it seems that it was never lost but spread geographically to displace the older, more primitive implement. Thus culture seems to have an evolution of its own, almost independent of the species evolution.

The characteristic of the first Acheulian flints was the chipping of both sides to produce a better-defined edge than was found on the earlier Oldowan implements that they superseded (Figure 12). Such bifacial finishing was not completely new to the Acheulian culture, however, as the late "Developed Oldowan" also showed flaking on both sides. The major innovations of the Acheulian culture consisted of a preference for flint over other stones, as well as the striking of a large flake from a flint nodule to use as a tool, rather than starting with a stone of approximately the right size. The flake was finished by a series of shallow flakings around the edges to produce a triangular outline with one sharp

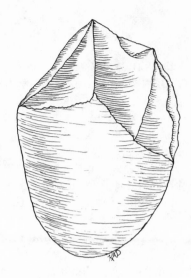

Figure 12. Oldowan "pebble tool," photograph and drawing. To make such a tool one merely selects a stone of the right size and knocks off a few flakes to produce a cutting edge. Even a beginner can produce one in less than two minutes. Compare these with the somewhat more refined Acheulian tools shown in Figure 13.

point, and two fairly straight edges, or, alternatively, an oval shape, sharpened all the way around (which seems foolish, as the tool would have been safer to use if one edge had been left unsharpened). Wooden handles for tools did not appear until much later in human history. There is no evidence of hafting of any of the stone implements of this period. The sharpened flints were evidently simply held in the hand and used as choppers, or "hand axes." The hand axe may be considered the most characteristic implement of the Acheulian culture (Figure 13). It could be used for piercing, cutting, or scraping. This basic tool showed remarkably little development over the entire period of several hundred thousand years. A slight refinement of workmanship is evident in the tools from more recent levels, but no technological "breakthroughs" are seen. Regional differences were probably more due to differences in the stone available than to changes in the tradition. When raw material was quarried from rock faces large flakes were used, rather than pebbles or nodules. Sometimes a square edge was formed in these large flakes, more like our modern idea of an axe blade.

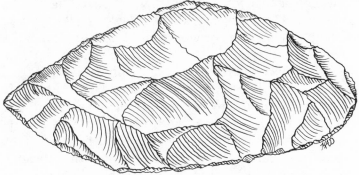

Figure 13. Acheulian hand axe. Although this implement is a great improvement over the Oldowan type, it is still a very primitive and crude artifact. "Axe" is somewhat misleading, for the sharpened stone was simply held in the hand and was probably used as much for cutting and scraping as for pounding or chopping. Variations in style of Acheulian tools were probably dictated more by the shape of the rock than by any conscious plan of the worker.

These special forms are known as cleavers. Probably the only progressive change one can trace is the greater use of flakes rather than pebbles as a starting point, and the gradual adoption of a thinner blade.

Other aspects of Acheulian culture remain largely hidden from archeologists. If spears or clubs were used, they were probably made of wood, and no trace has survived. Smaller flake tools, such as were used by later cultures to incise bone and wood implements, are not found. When the electron microscope is used to examine the edges of Acheulian blades, wear is seldom evident. Some anthropologists have been puzzled by this, but the most likely explanation is that *Homo erectus* did not value his possessions. He made his crude blades when he needed them, used them briefly for the job at hand, and then dropped them and moved on.

The organic evolution that transformed *Homo erectus* into Neanderthal man was fairly rapid, but we do not have enough fossils to give a detailed picture of the change. The cultural shift from Acheulian (associated with the last cultural stage of *Homo erectus*) to Mousterian is thought to reflect the emergence of Neanderthal, and so Mousterian flints are the earliest associated with *Homo sapiens*.

The Mousterian chronology traditionally covers the greater portion of the history of the classical Neanderthals but should not be completely equated with the Neanderthal subspecies. There had to be a transition both for the organic evolution from *erectus* to *neanderthalensis* and from the Acheulian to the Mousterian cultures, and the two shifts were not necessarily synchronized. At the other end of the time span, Mousterian culture developed into the Aurignacian as Neanderthal gave way to Cro-Magnon, but again the transition is not datable to a single point in time.

Until very recently the Mousterian culture was believed to have had its beginnings at the onset of the last glacial epoch, or at the end of the Riss–Würm interglacial, about 65,000 years ago, and to have lasted about 30,000 years. Recent evidence on the climatological changes of the last glacial periods has significantly changed our understanding of the time scale of the interglacial period. Instead of an abrupt cooling, the last interglacial period was followed by an interval that was neither fully interglacial nor yet glacial. That anomalous stage lasted fully 40,000 years and was finally terminated by a rather rapid onset of the glacial mode. This unexpected discovery doubles the time scale of the Mousterian culture! By the same token, Neanderthal evolution can be considered to have occurred at a much more leisurely pace than was believed. The transition from Acheulian to Mousterian now has to be placed at around 125,000 years ago (Figure 14).

The development of the flint tool technology we call Mousterian resulted from a gradual improvement of forms and techniques of the Acheulian (Figure 15). Although Mousterian is clearly an improvement over Acheulian, the transition shows no sign of an abrupt increase in the quality of intelligence or consciousness. Whenever really major improvements in technology have occurred in human history, they have tended to produce explosive cultural changes. There have been a number of jumps in cultural evolution, both in historic and prehistoric times. Specific discoveries in metallurgy had such great impact as to give the names "Bronze Age" and "Iron Age" to whole stages of human culture. More recently, the Industrial Revolution provides an excellent example of one such event. What can we learn from these recorded milestones in human history that might help us recognize the greatest jump of all, that unrecorded leap into linguistic competence that gave humans their first awareness of culture itself? Can we find any place in the dim fossil record of human evolution where a sudden discontinuity signals that leap?

Although in the long perspective of history cultural jumps appear quite abrupt, they were not necessarily a spectacular change for those living in the period. People who lived in the nineteenth century probably did not realize that they were in an Industrial Revolution until they looked back over many years of their lives. Revolutionary developments, like evolutionary changes, are rarely recognized as such while they are happening. As we go back in time, the fine details of an evolutionary change become blurred, and we see the transition as if it were much more drastic than it probably appeared to the people living through it. The development of agriculture, for example, doubtless took place over several generations. It consisted of many steps—finding plants that could be "domesticated," learning to clear and till the soil, inventing tools for harvesting and processing the crop—but from our present perspective the transition appears explosive, creating the greatest jump in cultural evolution we have found. Scarcely any phase of human activity was unaffected by the change from a nomadic, hunt-

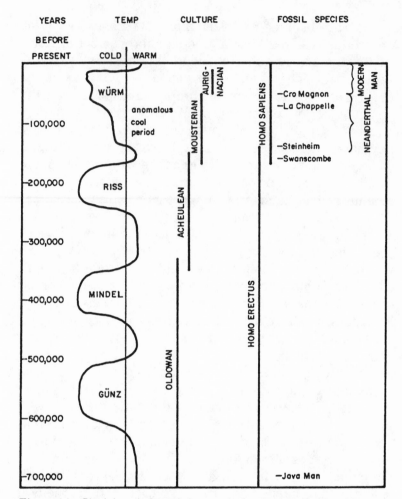

Figure 14. Glacial periods and time scale for the last stages of human evolution. The duration of the last interglacial period in this diagram reflects the very recent revision of the chronology of the Mousterian culture, largely based on worldwide ocean core sampling. This doubling of the span of time during which Neanderthals peopled the Earth gives more time for the transition into modern man but does not change our estimate of the time that the final transition took place.

ing, and gathering culture to a settled, home-building, and eventually city-building civilization.

The transition from Old Stone Age to New Stone Age or Neolithic culture is undoubtedly associated with the

Figure 15. Mousterian flint. These are
the cultural remains associated with the
Neanderthals. They are much more
complex and refined than Acheulian tools
but do not seem to indicate a qualitatively
different technology. Again, the culture
shows a surprising stability, with little
sign of innovation or impressive
improvement over a period of nearly
1,000 centuries. (Photographed at the
Musée de l'Homme, Paris.)

development of agriculture. Neolithic Man was fully modern
in all but his technology. We find it relatively easy to identify
with Neolithic peoples, many of whom have lived in historic
times. The American Indians, for instance, were in a
Neolithic culture stage when the first Europeans arrived on
this continent. Paleolithic culture, on the other hand, is almost impossible for us to imagine.

Agriculture, pottery, and metallurgy—each in its
turn transformed human life irreversibly. When we look at
the beautifully ornamented and skillfully finished stone implements of the Neolithic age, it is clear that the full development of mankind's artistic and technological abilities had
already arrived. Indeed, the splendid cave paintings of
southern France and Spain give eloquent testimony to a long
and fruitful tradition of graphic art antedating the Neolithic
period. But all of these accomplishments took place *after* the
development of human languages, which made rapid cultural evolution possible. Obviously the evolution of consciousness that this book attempts to describe was complete
long before the beginnings of the Neolithic age.

Most authorities agree that the final development of human intelligence took place sometime in the Upper Paleolithic period—within the last 100,000 years. The body of Cro-Magnon man is fully modern, whereas the physical form of Neanderthal, although clearly human, is not the light-limbed, "gracile" type we associate with a being who uses brains and technology instead of brute strength to survive. All the evidence points to the conclusion that the evolutionary jump into conscious humanity occurred among the "transitional Neanderthals," probably in the Near East, and almost surely within a few thousand years of the appearance of Cro-Magnon—perhaps about 50,000 years ago. We have seen the revolutionary effects on human life brought about by the later discoveries of our ancestors. Is there any sign of a corresponding cultural explosion to match this greatest step of all, the coming of language?

To decide this, let us look once more at the culture of the middle period "classical" Neanderthal, at the highest level of his pre-linguistic development. The Mousterian flint tools he used were usually made by striking flakes from a prepared core, followed by retouching on both sides. Retouching was achieved either by pounding or by "pressure flaking," which consisted of pushing down on the edges of the flint with a hard stick, bone, or antler until a small chip broke off. This method permitted greater precision and control of the retouching process than could be achieved by hammering. A typical tool might require the removal of a hundred additional chips for its final form.

Twelve to fifteen different tool types made up the usual Mousterian collection. The whole range of tools found in all sites combined would not be more than fifty or sixty different types. There is no good evidence for hafting. The flints were evidently held in the hand for use. As mentioned earlier, most of the flints show little or no evidence of wear. They were not valued as possessions, nor kept for long. This is partly explained by the ease and speed of their manufacture. We must not minimize the skill of these early people. I would not want to enter a flint-knapping contest with a Neanderthal. I am sure he could turn out a much better hand axe than I could, and in a fraction of the time. But the quality of consciousness displayed by the creation of a tool in this way is not impressive. The process is analytical rather than synthetic, in the literal Greek sense of those words: The tool already exists inside the flint nodule and requires only the removal of the excess stone to reveal its form. A later and higher order of conscious creation involved putting together or synthesizing different materials to create a complex structure that had no previous existence except in the imagination of its maker.

The great preponderance of "microliths" in the late Neanderthal and Cro-Magnon sites argues for a much more complex tool kit in which tiny blades were individually prepared and then assembled on a bone or wooden frame using a cement of pine pitch or other materials (Figure 16). Such implements could be used for sawing, for cutting, for preparing hides, or as weapons. The investment of time and effort was considerable, and these tools typically show much more wear. They were valued and retained. If the more perishable components of these relics had survived, it is likely that they would be decorated.

Neanderthal man did not master the art of working bone for tools. Bones were shattered, probably to obtain the marrow, but the paucity of burins among the flints argues that scribing or engraving on softer materials was not a common practice, as it became in successive cultures.

Figure 16. Microlith tools. After the static culture of the Mousterian deposits, the Cro-Magnon levels show a refreshing variety and exquisite workmanship. Microliths form a major share of the worked stone in most sites. These small, carefully shaped flints were assembled on a frame to make implements vastly more complex than anything in the Neanderthal tool kit.

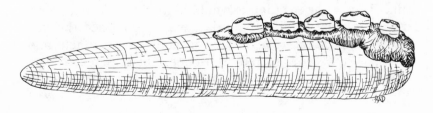

It seems likely that wood was used, but only a handful of wooden relics have survived the long years since Neanderthal vanished from the earth. A wooden spear that had been sharpened with a concave flint knife used as a spoke shave was found in a Paleolithic deposit in Essex, England. Another spear, from Saxony, seems to have had its tip hardened in a fire. A few "digging sticks" and a club complete the known inventory of what must be a tiny fraction of the wooden artifacts that once littered the living sites of early man.

Aside from hearths in cave sites, there is no evidence that Neanderthal built any structures. One site, near the Carpathian Mountains, revealed a large oval space containing many traces of cooking fires and surrounded by a ring of heavy mammoth bones. The arrangement suggests that the bones might have been used to hold down hides, forming a sort of hut. We cannot be sure; too many centuries have passed. The dating of the site is uncertain, but it must be older—perhaps much older—than 40,000 years.

Mousterian Neanderthals had not invented the needle, so they could not have made clothing, although many of their flints were evidently for the purpose of scraping hides.

Of the social organization and rituals of these late Neanderthals we know little. A few fossil sites provide what may be family groups of skeletons, which may suggest something of the ages and composition of such bands, but the number of known cases is too few for any statistically reliable evidence. Some of the skeletons show signs of deliberate burial and some evidence of ochre pigment, suggesting the possibility of ritual practices and even a belief in an afterlife. Again the sample is too small for any confident assessment.

So this was the state of man on the threshold of his final leap. How exciting it would be if we could uncover a record of that awakening! Alas, we have missed the moment. Excavations reveal layers of Mousterian artifacts, and then, abruptly, the incredible richness of the creativity of conscious man deposited above the older materials. We can estimate with increasing confidence the time when the leap happened, but we can only speculate on the event itself.

Speculation is not idle if it is based on broad knowledge and experience. Anthropologists, neuroscientists, and archeologists who have pondered these problems for years are finding an increased consensus about matters for which there is no direct physical evidence. An excellent example of informed speculation concerning the final evolutionary step into humanity was given by George Sacher in 1975. The idea that consciousness depended on a change in the basic mode of brain organization, rather than simply an increase in size, was startling when it first appeared, but by now the ideas are accepted almost casually by many workers. Sacher said:

> Man is not unique in the possession of a large brain. The elephants and numerous whale species have much larger brains, and several species of dolphins have brain:body ratios considerably higher than the pongids and not much below the human.

> I suggest that until about 100,000 years ago the hominids were in a neurophysiological situation very like those other species, in that comparatively complex traditions of hunting, migration, social organization, toolmaking, and environmental control were being implemented by comparatively inefficient nonsymbolic neural processes for learning, memory storage, and innovation, presumably based on highly evolved capacities for mental imagery, imitation, and dreaming. . . . At some point, a long series of pre- and proto-linguistic preadaptations coincided with the evolution of the brain to a critical size and resulted in the sudden—in evolutionary terms, almost instantaneous—invention of language. The resulting enormous increase in information processing capacity of the brain meant that as of that moment the amount of cortex was no longer the limiting factor in man's cognitive apprehension of his en-

vironment, so that, also as of that moment, selection for increased brain size ceased.[3]

Sacher is conservative in his dating, as he wrote before the revision of Neanderthal chronology. The development of language that he speaks of must have been just at the end of the Mousterian culture, when the linguistic capability conferred the final flowering of truly human culture upon the late Neanderthal.

If we are coming toward an agreement on the time of this event, can we also find the place where it happened? The best examples of "transitional Neanderthals" are the fossils from caves in the Near East. And there is one site that provides a remarkable hint: Shanidar.

Shanidar cave is in northern Iraq, near the Turkish border. It is in a moist valley leading down to the Greater Zab River, a tributary of the Tigris. Thus the "Fertile Crescent" of the Tigris and Euphrates is not only a cradle of civilization; it is quite possibly the site of the very dawn of human consciousness. The cave has been occupied by humans for about 100,000 years and is still occupied by a small band of Kurdish tribesmen. Ralph Solecki conducted an excavation of the cave, and in 1960, during the fourth season of his work, he uncovered a Neanderthal skeleton, later identified as that of a young male, in a niche between some large boulders. This was the fourth skeleton found, and so it was labeled "Shanidar IV." The bones were difficult to remove because of the cramped space they were in. Fortunately Solecki took soil samples from several places in and around the skeleton for later pollen analysis. The bones were then sprayed with plastic and covered with wet newspaper. Plaster of paris was poured over the whole mass, so that it could be removed intact. The soil samples were taken almost casually, since there was no reason to expect anything special about this layer of the excavation.

It was two years before the bones were studied, and still later before the pollen analysis was begun. When the samples were examined for pollen content—a procedure that gives information about the season and the climate at the time the deposit was formed—a strange thing was noted. Usually fossil pollen grains are found scattered widely among the grains of soil, where they had been blown in ancient times by the wind. They represent a very random sample of the plants that flowered in the vicinity of the cave mouth. In the Shanidar samples, incredible numbers of pollen grains of the same species were found in the same small sample. The interpretation was that these were not wind-blown pollen grains but the remains of whole flowers that had been buried at the same time as the corpse. Later investigations of the same material revealed that no less than eight different types of flowers were represented, all brightly colored, and all blooming in late spring. Among the eight were a yellow groundsel, grape hyacinth, yarrow, a blue bachelor's button, rose mallow, and hollyhock. The conclusion seems inescapable: Someone had laid that young man's body to rest on a bed of brightly colored flowers, deliberately gathered. Wild hollyhocks do not grow in clumps, so the number represented by the pollen clusters would require that they be plucked over a wide area.

Other Late Neanderthal skeletons have seemed to indicate the possibility that "grave goods" were deliberately placed with the body, but the number of such finds is too few to rule out accidental proximity, or that the individual died suddenly with his belongings at his side. No other site than Shanidar speaks to us with such poignancy. By the standards of human history 60,000 years is an unspeakably long time, but across even the chasm the flowers of Shanidar capture the imagination and provide the most convincing evidence we have that Late Neanderthal had crossed the threshold of consciousness to the extent of recognizing death, and of providing some sort of consoling ritual to cope with the dread and sorrow that such recognition entails.

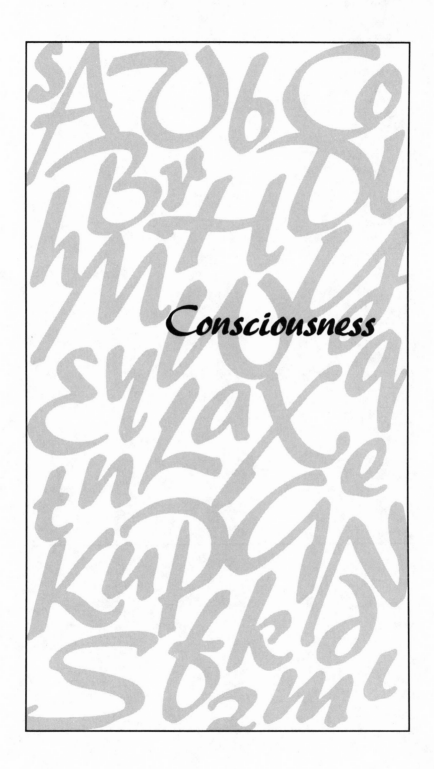

Consciousness

In the beginning was the Word.
JOHN 1:1

CONSCIOUSNESS, in the sense I wish to use the word, is not only unique to humans—it is the distinguishing feature that *defines* humanity and separates us from all other animals. *Human consciousness* is almost synonymous with *language*. The linguistic capability of our brain is intimately involved in all of our awareness, memory, imagination, and knowledge. We think in words and symbols. Hence an explanation of how consciousness arose is an explanation of the evolution of language. It follows that the transition from beast to human was triggered by the evolutionary step that gave the brain its linguistic capacity. When and how this crucial evolutionary step occurred can now, perhaps for the first time, be examined with some confidence. It happened very recently—probably within the last 100,000 years. All of the evidence suggests that it happened suddenly. There had to be a final breakthrough. A sudden awakening.

Any examination of the basic nature of consciousness is hindered by the impossibility of stripping off all the rich accumulations of cultural influences. No human mind is a *tabula rasa* free of learning, connotations, associations. By the time an infant has developed to the stage where his or her brain has the capability of language, that infant has already been subjected to a pervasive cultural indoctrination.

In the same way it is difficult to study the basic characteristics of human linguistics, since every human whom we can interrogate has already learned a specific language and a specific grammar. We would like to be able to compare an immediate "before" and an "after" condition to see what the evolution of consciousness had accomplished. This is forever beyond our grasp; we have come too far from the pristine state of human mentality that existed immediately after consciousness was born. Once the linguistic capability was found, the human mind was caught up in a rushing tide of cultural evolution that has swept us so far that any human child who is old enough to speak is already removed an unimaginable distance from that first dawning.

The "before" is equally inaccessible. Studying other animal species is of little use. Our most immediate subhuman ancestor was already the product of a long evolutionary path of bipedalism, tool using, and proto-linguistic patterns that no other animal has ever followed. He was farther removed from the chimpanzee than a fine Swiss watch is from a crude sundial. All of the hominid lines are extinct except ours, and in our species consciousness is so profoundly conditioned by our linguistic past that it cannot be bared for examination.

To discuss the evolution of consciousness we must try to define it in terms of its biological (that is, neurological) elements. There are several ways of approaching the problem. We can trace the evolution of the human brain and point to the particular developments that led to a linguistic mode of neural processing. Comparison with other animals also gives some help, for the brain, like any other organ, evolved by the modification and extension of existing parts, not by the abrupt addition of new structures. Insofar as the anatomical study of the brain can provide information as to its function, comparative anatomy is relevant. But there is a severe limitation to the amount we can deduce about function when studying pickled nervous tissue.

If we turn to living brains, lower animals provide the bulk of our experimental evidence, since drastic experimentation on human brains is not possible. Although we have learned a great deal about the elementary functions of nerve cells by study of living tissue in the squid, the laboratory rat, and other vertebrates and invertebrates, there is an obvious limit to the extent to which such studies can illuminate those higher functions of the nervous system that are restricted to the human race.

Clinical experience from medical treatment of human patients provides the best evidence we have about the mechanisms of the higher mental functions. Records of the neurological symptoms resulting from specific brain injuries or abnormalities go back as far as 3000 B.C. The Edward Smith Papyrus, a surgical treatise written at the beginning of the first Egyptian dynasty, reveals a considerable degree of sophistication regarding brain specialization and the anatomical location of certain sensory and motor control areas. In the many centuries since then, innumerable cases of neurological disorders have been studied. Taken collectively, such evidence does provide a substantial body of knowledge about the functional organization of the human brain, even without the possibility of deliberate laboratory experimentation on human subjects.

None of these approaches provides a clear explanation of the biological basis of consciousness. The "ghost in the machine" has eluded both the clinician and the basic research scientist. Perhaps by examining the evolution of the symbolic processing mechanisms that made language possible we can unravel the tangled thread of consciousness itself.

It is always tempting to seek a single cause and a single explanation for any phenomenon. If we accept that the acquisition of language/consciousness was the necessary and sufficient event for the evolutionary jump from beast to human, we want to know what *particular* development in the brain was responsible for that crucial step.

If we were trying to explain the evolution of flight, we would first have to explain the several changes that led to the structure of a wing. Without wings, flight is impossible.

But flightless creatures have no use for wings. What then was the guiding principle that could lead the front limbs through the slow adaptive changes toward a wing? The changes could not have occurred all at once. Yet there must have been a last crucial step that made the difference between flight and non-flight. A satisfactory description of that step would have to include the necessary preliminary adaptations and the mechanism that accounted for the whole process.

Similarly for the evolution of consciousness. There had to be a final jump into consciousness, but there also had to be a whole train of preadaptations to ready the brain for this new kind of function. The nature of these preadaptations can largely be deduced, and why they occurred can also be plausibly explained. The explanation does not invoke the argument of selection for adaptive advantage in the simplistic way that the principle has often been applied. No evolutionary adaptation involving a qualitative stepwise change can be based on that argument. What selective pressure could lead to the gradual changes from a front leg to a wing? A wing is useless unless you fly with it, but you can't fly until the slow changes are completed. Nor is it likely that a sudden mutation should provide, at one stroke, a functional wing. The problem with tracing an evolutionary progression is that every intermediate stage has to have its own logic and justification. Selection does not operate on hope. The intermediate stages between a front leg and a wing had to have their own valid uses, or such a path would not have been followed. Feathers probably evolved for insulation to go along with the warm-bloodedness of the transitional dinosaurs that were to become birds. Feathers have become essential for bird flight, although not for flight in general, as bats and insects manage without them. Some kind of jumping, gliding, or sailing, in which the front limbs were used as aerodynamic rudders to provide lift and stability, but that did not compromise their use in other ways, may have permitted the stepwise evolutionary changes in the bone and muscle structures that then became useful for a new purpose.

The foregoing example is not a very accurate description of the evolution of flight. A technological development can be recounted more accurately. We can point to an exact moment when Orville and then Wilbur Wright took off on that December morning on the first powered flight. The transition from gliding, sailing, or jumping to true flight was probably less abrupt in the biological case than in human technology. Nevertheless, there was, in both instances, a "preadaptation" for sailing or gliding, followed by a transition into powered flight.*

The biological mechanism that is invoked to explain stepwise evolutionary advances such as these has been called *preadaptation*. As the name implies, the changes are already in place when the need arises. What caused the changes in the first place must be explained in terms of some other need. A better term for this kind of evolutionary process is *exaptation*. The need finds the structure, like a solution finding a problem. Biologists eschew a mystical explanation for the apparent logic in biological structure. "God's plan" is a comforting belief for the miraculous order and beauty of nature, but such a belief should not substitute for scientific exploration of the rational principles that govern our universe.

To satisfactorily explain the evolution of a wing or a capacity for consciousness requires that we find other useful functions that might have directed the evolutionary selection of those organs for a more immediate purpose. Selection

*Some biologists propose that the evolution of flight in the vertebrates occurred in running and leaping rather than gliding forms. Two-legged dinosaurs are well known. Perhaps, they say, some small insect-eating two-legged dinosaurs developed aerodynamic structures from their front limbs to help control their landing from the leaps they made in pursuit of their insect prey. Such appendages might then become powerful enough to provide actual lift. The major selective advantage that directed the evolution of wings, according to this theory, was the improved efficiency and control they provided for a running and jumping animal, rather than an increase in the range of a glide. Wilbur and Orville Wright might have appreciated this theory. They were convinced that the major secret of powered flight lay in developing a means of *controlling* the flying machine, rather than in providing a source of power. Most of their experimentation was directed toward that end, and each of them had many hours of "flight time" in their gliders before they finally, almost casually, added an engine to their airframe.

can operate only when there is a present advantage. Since it is unlikely that an arm became a wing by one enormous re-ordering of its structure, one must find uses for each of the small changes that must have taken place over many generations. Without such uses, the transitional individuals would not have survived in competition with their fellows. *Preadaptation* is not a very satisfactory name for this process. It tends to imply that the adaptation was directed toward the specific goal, whereas in fact the ultimate function arose, as it were, by accident, when a new use was found for a structure that had developed in response to a different need. Once the new function is established, it often leads to a period of very rapid additional changes in the structures involved, as the selection process can now, at last, operate on the final function. This may explain many cases of evolutionary jumps.

A fine modern explanation of this process is given in a famous paper, "The Spandrels of San Marco and the Panglossian Paradigm: a Critique of the Adaptationist Programme" by S. J. Gould and R. C. Lewontin. The paper begins with a description of the splendid mosaics of St. Mark's Cathedral:

> The great central dome of St. Mark's Cathedral in Venice presents in its mosaic design a detailed iconography expressing the mainstays of Christian faith. Three circles of figures radiate out from a central image of Christ: angels, disciples, and virtues. Each circle is divided into quadrants, even though the dome itself is radially symmetrical in structure. Each quadrant meets one of the four spandrels in the arches below the dome. Spandrels—the tapering rectangular spaces formed by the intersection of two rounded arches at right angles—are necessary architectural by-products of mounting a dome on rounded arches. Each spandrel contains a design admirably fitted into its tapering space. An evangelist sits in the

upper part flanked by the heavenly cities. Below, a man representing one of the four Biblical rivers (Tigris, Euphrates, Indus, and Nile) pours water from a pitcher into the narrowing space below his feet.

The design is so elaborate, harmonious and purposeful that we are tempted to view it as the starting point for any analysis, as the cause in some sense of the surrounding architecture. But this would invert the proper path of analysis. The system begins with an architectural constraint: the necessary four spandrels and their tapering triangular form. They provide a space in which the mosaicists worked; they set the quadripartite symmetry of the dome above.[4]

The authors go on to explain that the "adaptationist programme" is a "Panglossian paradigm" after Voltaire's Dr. Pangloss, who believed that everything was made for the best purpose. Spectacles need to be supported, and we have noses; breeches were clearly intended to cover legs, and we have legs!

Poor Dr. Pangloss is a ridiculous figure. We all recognize that his logic is backwards. It is less clear that many biological adaptations are "explained" by a similar reversal of cause and effect. The power of Darwin's insight about natural selection has led to its misapplication as a universal explanation of every biological adaptation. Seeing a useful structure, the adaptationist makes the sometimes simplistic assumption that nature has brought about the development of that structure for its present purpose through the operation of the principle of Darwinian selection. This way of thinking ignores the possibility that serendipity operates in nature as well as in the affairs of men, and that often a new and "unintended" use is found for a structure that evolved for quite different reasons. The nose *is* a useful support for spectacles, but nobody but Dr. Pangloss would suppose that the mechanisms for evolution had been directed toward providing noses for that purpose. A button on the forehead might have served better.

To avoid a Panglossian explanation of the evolution of consciousness we must seek an adaptive value for the intermediate changes in the brain that eventually made the linguistic and conscious functions possible. If consciousness, like flight, is a stepwise evolutionary advance, it seems likely that the necessary adaptations of the brain were not selected for on the basis of their future value, but rather for some immediate utility.

The alternative scenario, which has been assumed by most of the writers on this topic, is that human consciousness developed as a consequence of language (rather than as a correlate) and that language evolved, according to an adaptationist program, as a result of the selective advantage of increasingly complex communication between individuals. No one would deny the plausibility of this hypothesis. Certainly it is obvious that speech is likely to be an important asset to a social and cooperative animal. A major problem (though not the only difficulty) with this adaptationist program is that it does not suggest any neurological mechanism for the actual evolutionary changes in the brain necessary for a language faculty. It is a Panglossian paradigm in that it says "language is useful, and behold, we have a brain with linguistic capability."

Language, in the sense of communication between individuals, did not direct the evolution of a greater and greater linguistic capacity of the brain, any more than spectacles directed the evolution of the human nose. Certainly pre-linguistic hominids communicated with one another, just as troops of baboons or packs of wolves do. But the full richness of human speech did not develop until the drastic reordering of the human brain made possible a new quality of symbolic processing.

In fact, the capacity for language was perhaps the last major step in our biological evolution, for it sparked such a torrent of cultural invention that the history of human evolution since that time has been completely dominated by cultural, rather than biological, advances.

The biological evolution of language means simply the development of a mental capacity for the manipulation of information in the form of a general symbolic code. A neurological explanation of the evolution of language has to begin with a distinction between language, which is a biological capability, and *a* language, which is a cultural artifact. When we view language as a physiological rather than a cultural phenomenon, one insight to emerge is that the pattern of information processing is determined by the mechanisms that the brain has evolved, not by a set of agreed-upon rules. Thus there is a universal syntax that dictates the grammar of every invented language, as suggested by Noam Chomsky. It ought to be possible to discover this "universal grammar" even when it is hidden in particular rules that may have been "artificially" developed in a specific language.

A belief in a universal syntax is subtly implied by the expectation that any language can be translated into any other. It is difficult to imagine a language that is so different from all other human languages that translation is literally impossible. Even in the search for extraterrestrial intelligence there is an unexamined assumption that other intelligent beings would have evolved the same logical rules that govern human discourse.

Language can be divided into two major components, *vocabulary* and *syntax*. Vocabulary is simply a code— an agreed-upon set of symbols that stand for the components (nouns, verbs, adjectives, etc.) that make up a specific language. In the language of mathematics it is the numbers themselves, and a set of symbols—a "plus" or a "minus" sign, or an integral sign—that indicate the operations to be performed on the numbers; in sign language, it is the gestures. Syntax is much more profound. It is the operating rules for manipulating the elements of the vocabulary to produce a meaningful message. One might understand the symbols

$$(36/12)^3 = ?$$

but if the rules of long division and raising to a power were not understood, the problem could not be solved. In a curious way, syntax tends to be invisible. Because of the universality of human syntax, the problem of fundamental grammar can often be ignored when one translates or "decodes" a foreign language. Even though rules of sequence vary, a readable translation of a coded message can usually be made by simply substituting the appropriate vocabulary, word for word. Try to imagine a language so different in its underlying syntax that even if the words themselves were understood, the message would be meaningless to a human. It is difficult. It is even difficult to make up meaningless combinations of words in our own language, such is the power of our innate syntax to impose a logic and order on our symbols. The "sentence" "Why is a duck that spins," although nonsensical at first glance, can be stretched to provide some sort of meaning if only by partially violating the particular rules of English grammar. " 'Why' is (the name of) a duck that spins." "Why is (there) a duck that spins (?)"

If syntax is innate, it is closely related to other innate systems that give us the mental capacities for logic, arithmetic, and other cognitive functions. If these systems are the result of a particular biological capability of the human brain, the possibility exists that a different evolutionary quirk might have led to a different kind of system—an alternative arithmetic, a different logic. Many philosophers have wrestled with the question of whether systems of logic (and of mathematics) are universal. Do they exist as eternal truths, independently of our human grasp of their principles, or are they simply inventions of our mind that happen to "work" in terms of being consistent with the apparent operations of our universe? One aspect of this problem is the question of relativity (not especially in the Einsteinian sense). Newton assumed an absolute space and a set of fixed laws governing the universe. Leibnitz embraced a more relativistic view, in which nature was somehow affected by our particular apprehension of it. The Newton–Leibnitz dichotomy obsessed eighteenth-century philosophers. Euler favored Newton's view, and Kant, perhaps influenced by Euler, wrote his famous work asserting the doctrine of absolute space and absolute laws which we can apprehend *a priori*, through the universal power of all human minds to recognize logical truth.

Many contemporary philosophers embrace a more relativistic view of logic and the laws of nature. One can suggest, without running the risk of being accused of mysticism, that physical laws and the properties of our universe are somewhat influenced by our perceptions, and that alternative views are conceivable. Where Kant regarded logic as a single, immutable, universal system, modern philosophers recognize a plurality of logics.

Syntax, like logic, is a set of rules that form a system with its own internal structure and laws. Humans can discover those rules, but we are not free to make up any set of arbitrary rules and have them apply validly within the system. Euclidean geometry is another such system. Euclid did not invent the rules governing the relationships between the angles of a triangle. He discovered them. Nevertheless, there can be non-Euclidean geometries with different sets of rules, and these, too, are internally consistent and not susceptible to arbitrary "legislation."

Stretch your mind and try to imagine a "non-Euclidean syntax" with which a language could be constructed. The rules of grammar would be logical, consistent, and orderly, but the messages generated by that grammar would be totally incomprehensible in our "Euclidean" syntax, just as the statement "parallel lines never meet," which is quite reasonable in Euclidean geometry, is nonsense in some non-Euclidean systems. The neurological structures which make human language possible evolved only once, and we all share the same syntax. But the difficulty of imagining an alternative syntax should not blind us to the possibility that other reasonable systems could have evolved, or that they may exist on other worlds. It is conceivable that the messages our radiotelescopes are listening for from extraterrestrial civilizations will be forever untranslatable.

There are many human languages, but all of them are based on one universal syntax. Invention of a human language is like the invention of a machine. There are many

ways that it can be done, but infinitely more ways that it cannot be done, for some rules must be obeyed. Throwing a set
of gears, levers, screws, and bits of metal into a box and
shaking them up is not likely to produce a usable mechanism. In making up a new language or a code, one has to
follow the rules of human syntax or one will produce gibber-
ish. Syntax is the *mechanism* that directs the manipulation of
the symbols that make up the vocabulary. The symbols can
be combined to produce an infinite variety of messages, but
the combinations are orderly, not random.

Although syntax is obviously central to linguistic
competence, its relationship to consciousness is not yet
clear. "A syntactic capability" is not a satisfactory definition
of consciousness. For one thing, if we accept the near iden-
tity between language and consciousness, defining the first
in terms of the second would be circular. But more important, syntax, although it has been studied intensively for
many years, is practically impossible to define. David Premack, in an article entitled "Language and Intelligence in
Apes and Man," describes the difficulty:

> Human syntax is marvelously, even wondrously,
> complex. There is no more powerful logical sys-
> tem on earth. Of all the systems man has managed
> to invent—maths, logics, artificial/computer lan-
> guages—none can be used to describe human lan-
> guage, whereas human language can be used to
> describe all other systems. The system that
> grows naturally from the human brain is more po-
> tent than any system man has been able to culti-
> vate self-consciously.[5]

This system that Premack says "grows naturally from the
human brain" is no less than the mechanism for *manipulating* the symbols in an orderly way to produce meaning. That
might almost do as a definition of consciousness. If consciousness is the power to generate mental experiences by
organizing symbols in some neural code, what are the characteristics of this process that might be studied "from the

outside," as it were? Once we have identified the objective signs of consciousness, perhaps we can explore the neurological mechanisms that might be responsible for this ability.

Neither of these tasks is easy. An "objective" analysis of human consciousness is almost a paradox. To make such an analysis we could employ what might be called a Skinnerian paradigm, after B. F. Skinner, who reacted against the introspective psychology of the nineteenth century by declaring that the brain must be treated as a "black box" that we are forbidden to open. He declared that the only way to avoid subjectivism in studying the brain is to examine the behavior in terms of input–output transformations. We should describe what actually happens and not try to guess what inner mechanisms are responsible. Skinner would prefer that we say, "rewards reinforce behavior, punishment reduces it" rather than "The rat wants food and tries to avoid electric shocks."

This is perhaps an unfairly simplistic description of the Skinnerian approach, which has merit in that it suggests that consciousness should be identifiable by external signs, without recourse to the redundancy inherent in asking consciousness to examine itself.

The subject of this discussion is *human* consciousness. Obviously a sleeping cat lacks something that is present in a cat that is awake, and the word we use for this something is *consciousness*. But the consciousness we are attempting to examine is much more than the opposite of unconsciousness. The phenomenon exhibited by a cat that is awake is a far cry from the rich inner stream of experience enjoyed by a human. Animal lovers often object to any suggestion that pets differ fundamentally from humans in their mental state. Innumerable anecdotes are told to prove that the "lower" animals are practically human in their emotional, cognitive, and sometimes moral qualities. What then are the peculiar elements of human consciousness that can be recognized by an outside observer and that are demonstrably different from that lesser kind of "consciousness" enjoyed by any nonsleeping animal? I suggest the following:

CONSCIOUSNESS

1. *Self-Recognition* (often called *self-consciousness*). Child psychologists agree on the importance of the development of the idea of self in an infant. Clinical experience with patients suffering from derangements of their ego identification shows the importance of self-recognition in the human psyche. Even recognizing one's self in a mirror is one facet of this capacity. Self-recognition, like other aspects of human consciousness, may not be totally lacking in the lower animals. Although dogs, for example, sometimes show interest in their own reflections, it is not clear just what they think they are seeing.

2. *Volition.* Neglecting the philosophical debate about free will, it is obvious that humans are capable of initiating thoughts or activities independently of any obvious external stimulus. In a trivial sense lower animals do this too, but the degree by which humans have emancipated themselves from dependence on immediate environmental cues as a motive for action clearly points to volition as a distinctly human faculty.

3. *Pattern Recognition.* A human, after solving a maze with a regular pattern, will be able to solve any equivalent maze immediately. All other animals tested in this (to us) easy task fail completely. Each new case must be completely relearned. This property is related to the more general issue of cognitive mapping, of which more will be said later.

4. *Generalization* and *Abstraction.* This property should not be confused with simple induction, which some lower animals do very well. Generalization, the ability to perceive essential attributes independently of the contingencies of a specific case, and to categorize, enables us to comprehend relationships among phenomena. In daily use it is a major element in what we call "understanding." It is a complex feat that even humans often do poorly: It took a Newton to perceive the law of gravity in the fall of an apple.

5. *Intermodal Association.* This is a special case of generalization, but one of enormous importance, since it lies at the very heart of language. Intermodal association means the ability to combine the information from two or more sen-

sory modalities into one meaning. It has taken many years of frustrating failures to convince most psychologists that lower animals entirely lack this faculty, which seems so easy and effortless to humans. Experimental animals never learn to associate the louder of two tones, for example, with the brighter of two lights. Each sensory system is isolated and independent.

A list of some of the external attributes of the conscious mind is only the first step of an analysis; it does little to explain the special properties of the human brain that make language and consciousness possible. What are those properties?

The first, and most obvious, is the sheer amount and complexity of the cerebral cortex. But size and complexity are not enough in themselves. As pointed out by Sacher in the passage quoted in Chapter One, man is not alone in having a large and complex brain. Obviously a certain minimum amount of neural circuitry is necessary to support a human-type intellectual faculty, but evidently the amount of gray matter in our brain is far greater than that minimum. Horrendous injuries involving a major fraction of the cerebral cortex can leave the victim, after recovery, with an almost unimpaired intelligence. Within the last few years a certain Cambridge University undergraduate was examined for persistent headaches; X-ray studies revealed that a hydrocephalic condition in his infancy had produced a compression of the cerebral tissue, leaving him with only about one-tenth of the normal volume of gray matter. Yet he was a brilliant student, and nobody had ever suspected the extent of his cortical deficiency because his intellectual functions were very satisfactory.

If size and complexity alone are insufficient to account for the unique capacity for language found in the human brain, we must look for some special pattern of organization that differs from the circuitry of other animal brains and confers the precious gift of consciousness on our species. What can we discover by objective examination that distinguishes the organization of the human brain from that of all other animals?

Two features stand out. The first is the bilateral specialization of the cerebral hemispheres. The human cerebrum is unusual not only for its large size, but also for the fact that the two halves have developed somewhat different functions. All vertebrates have an obvious kind of lateral specialization in that each half of the brain serves half of the body in its motor and sensory functions. Humans have added to this relatively trivial sort of specialization a completely new kind of right–left differentiation of function that is just beginning to be explored scientifically.

Bilateral specialization of the cerebrum is very closely associated with the language function. In the study of brain functions it was discovered quite early that only one side of the brain controlled speech. Right- or left-handedness is now recognized to be a reflection of one aspect of motor dominance, which is also related to the hemispheric differentiation. Geometric skills are controlled by one side; numerical calculations by the other. "Artistic" capabilities are on the opposite side from "analytic" functions. It is unfortunate that the word *dominance* came to be associated with the phenomenon of hemispheric differentiation, for we now recognize that the "nondominant" hemisphere is, in fact, better at many mental tasks. The lateral specialization of the cerebrum will be discussed in Chapter Four.

The second unusual feature of the human brain is that it has a special form of neural processing for which we have no satisfactory name, but that has been described by such terms as *holographic, statistical,* and *nondeterministic.* The "holographic" mode of cerebral organization is perhaps the essence of human consciousness. It is undoubtedly the most difficult mechanism to explain. A fuller discussion will be presented in Chapter Four, but for now let us look at some major characteristics of the process.

1. It is not deterministic. That is, knowledge of the pattern of neuronal connections in the brain does not enable one to

predict the outcome of a stimulus applied to the neurons in the network.

2. It is not localizable. The activity is "global" in that it involves large areas of the cerebral hemispheres. In general, damage to any specific area of the brain will not destroy the function.

3. It is superimposable on other types of neuronal activity. Many neurons of the cerebrum are involved in more specific, deterministic functions, such as sensory reception or movement control, in addition to their participation in the holographic activity of consciousness. The two classes of activity do not interfere with each other.

4. It is totally interconnected. Information can be transferred from any location in the cerebrum to any other. (Think of memory. How do you retrieve a specific memory of some past event? You can get to it by an enormous number of pathways: association with a specific person, a time, a place, a certain smell or taste. The possibilities are endless, so vast is your cross-filing system.)

These two characteristics, bilateral specialization of the cerebrum and a holographic mode of information processing, are central to the development of the capability for language and consciousness. If we follow this thread, looking for signs of their emergence in the primitive brain, we may be led to a better understanding of how and why consciousness evolved in our Neanderthal ancestors.

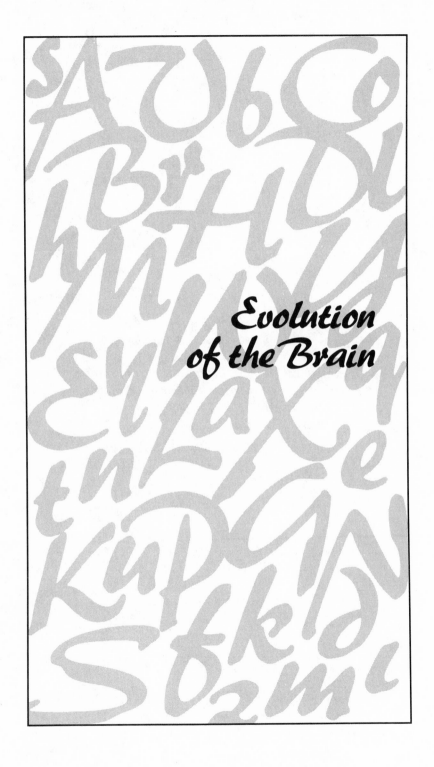

Evolution
of the Brain

It seems, as one becomes older,
That the past has another pattern,
and ceases to be a mere sequence—
Or even development: the latter a partial fallacy,
Encouraged by superficial notions of evolution,
Which becomes, in the popular mind,
a means of disowning the past.

T. S. ELIOT[6]

LANGUAGE IS A DISTINCTIVELY HUMAN characteristic that separates us from all other animals, but language could not have evolved without a brain capable of complex symbolic processing. To understand the biological basis of language and consciousness we must understand how the brain functions. Human brains are so extraordinarily complex that it is very difficult to sort out the various mechanisms that make complex symbolic processing possible. We will be better able to trace these functions if we start with simpler brains from which our own have evolved. For this reason we must begin at a much earlier stage of vertebrate evolution than we have considered so far. The vertebrate brain has a history that goes back several hundred million years, so the time scale of this discussion is much longer than the few hundred thousand years considered in Chapter One.

For a biologist used to thinking in terms of evolution it is not surprising to find similarities among different groups of animals. High-school biology classes dissect frogs to learn more about human body structures, for frogs and humans have hearts, stomachs, and other organs that are clearly similar. Both the frog and the human have descended from more primitive animals that had hearts and stomachs, and although these organs have certainly changed with our different needs, the close similarities in form and function make it easy to trace the evolutionary connections. The frog's heart is an acceptable model for studying our own. But not all of the similar adaptations we find in different life forms have this evolutionary relationship. Sometimes unrelated animal species develop structures that appear similar but that do not derive from any common ancestral precursor.

The independent evolution of closely similar organs looks to us like re-inventing the wheel. A familiar case is that of the vertebrate eye and the eye of the squid. Both are spherical chambers filled with fluid. They each have a sensitive retina, a lens, and a large optic nerve connecting the retina to the brain. They even function alike in the way they process the visual information for transmission in the "code" of nerve impulses. Yet the animal phylum to which the squid belongs (the mollusks) is so remotely related to the vertebrates that we know there can be no direct evolutionary connection between the squid's eye and our own. These two remarkably similar structures had to arise independently of each other.

If you look closely at certain species of moth you will find that their bodies are covered with a "fur" that looks and feels exactly like that of a mouse, a fox, or any furry mammal. Yet, as in the case of the eye of the squid, the "fur" of insects is not directly related through any possible evolutionary pathway to the fur of mammals. Many such cases of independent evolution of similar adaptations have been observed—too many to be explained away as coincidence. Biologists are uneasy about such similarities when the underlying guiding principle is not apparent.

The organizing pattern of animal nervous systems provides many examples of these disturbing coincidences. The largest taxonomic group, other than kingdom, is the phylum. The animal kingdom is divided into some thirty different phyla. Some, like the sponges, are extremely simple and seem remote from our usual notion of "animals." Since each phylum has evolved separately from all the others over a period of time measured in the hundreds of millions of years, the genetic relationships between, say, an oyster and a mosquito, or a snake and an angleworm are remote and tenuous. Yet despite the long evolutionary history that separates each animal phylum from all the others, every animal that has a brain exhibits a number of noticeably similar adaptations. The cellular mechanisms of neurons are essentially identical in all of the different groups. Neural circuits show the same patterns, and even the wide range of different chemical substances that function as neurotransmitters is remarkably consistent in the different phyla. Animals from groups as diverse as mollusks, annelids, arthropods, vertebrates, and even the microscopic nematodes can be used for experiments on the nervous system, and the experimenters have confidence that most of their findings will be of general validity beyond the particular species they find convenient to work with.

Within our own phylum, the vertebrates, of course one expects to find somewhat greater conformity, since we all share a common evolutionary relationship. But even here the pattern seems more consistent and conservative than one expects, given the wide range of variability in other body features as one goes from fish to bird, or from platypus to tiger. Perhaps because of this conservatism, the nervous system provides some of the best evidence for evolutionary development that we can find. One can trace a logical evolutionary pathway of ever-increasing complexity and size as we look at the brains of representative species of vertebrates, going from the most primitive to the most recent.

The implications of this mysterious conformity of neural structure both within our own phylum and, more especially, between distantly related animals from separate phyla, are intriguing. Unless there is some completely unsuspected direct evolutionary link between these widely separated groups of animals, we have to accept that the close similarities of pattern are a problem. They violate our estimates of the probability that several independent sequences would lead to such a uniform outcome. The theory of evolution holds that variations in structures arise randomly, rather than by some directing mechanism. After the random changes take place, the adaptive principle determines which shall be retained and which shall be culled out by the well-known mechanism of "survival of the fittest." If the original variations are indeed random, then it seems highly unlikely that such a mechanism should hit upon the same pattern of neural structures again and again. One way out of this quandary is simply to embrace a teleological explanation as an end to inquiry: "There is a destiny which shapes our ends. . . ." Scientists, whether or not they believe in a Divine Providence, prefer to seek a scientific explanation for the material phenomena of our universe. To invoke a *deus ex machina* for every unexplained mystery is not playing the game. It not only violates the rules of science, but it denigrates religion as well. If an explicit miraculous intervention is required for the day-to-day operation of our mundane world, what reaction can we have left over for the truly awesome descent of an archangel? "Hi, Gabriel. What's new?"

To eschew a teleological explanation of evolution is not to deny God. The gospel says, "That which is born of the flesh is flesh, and that which is born of the spirit is spirit." Biologists deal with the flesh. They believe that, like all other aspects of our created universe, living organisms are designed rationally, and reason should be able to discern the logic of the pattern without resorting to mysticism.

So, if we rule out the miraculous, what explanation can we find for the uncanny recurrence of the same pattern again and again in evolutionary adaptations? Two possibilities present themselves, and both of them have useful implications as we seek to understand how the brain developed its linguistic capacity. The first one is that the number of reasonable solutions to a given problem of adaptation is much more limited than we imagine, so that even random processes are very likely to arrive at the same goal over and over. The second is that some underlying mechanism common to all neurons predisposes them toward certain limited patterns of organization among the many potential possibilities.

If we examine the first of the two proposed explanations we can find plausible analogies among the many cases of "convergence" found in human inventions that, though not consciously modeled on natural mechanisms, frequently turn out to be close copies of the pattern worked out by evolution. The camera is a device very similar to the eye, and it is hard to imagine a better way of projecting an image onto a sensitive surface. Likewise, color photography and color television are also examples of unintentional plagiarism of the mechanisms nature had long ago developed for color vision. Spiders, moths, and the DuPont Corporation have all arrived independently at almost identical mechanisms for converting a fluid substance into long threads. The chemical composition of rayon differs from that of silk, but the spinnerettes have much the same structure, and the mechanism for extruding the viscous fluid to form the threads is very similar.

These examples suggest that some problems may have only one reasonable solution. In such cases, the fact that independent pathways lead to the same final mechanism is not surprising. However, not all of our biological examples seem explainable in this way, and so we must explore the second possibility—that there may be underlying principles inherent in the living cell that give a pattern and direction to the development of new structures. Neurotransmitters provide a good example of this second possibility, but some background explanation is required.

Whenever you wiggle your toe, or when you hear a sound or touch a hot stove, your muscles and your sense organs communicate with your brain by means of electrical waves traveling down the nerves. Nerve impulses travel from the cell body of the neuron down the long fibers called axons. Each axon ends in a set of small bulbs called terminal buttons, containing a chemical agent called a neurotransmitter. When the impulse arrives at the terminal button, a small quantity of the neurotransmitter is released. The chemical diffuses rapidly across the synapse (the point at which two neurons make contact, and through which the activity of the pre-synaptic neuron is transferred to the post-synaptic neuron). The action of the neurotransmitter chemical on the membrane of the post-synaptic neuron is what delivers the excitatory or inhibitory "message" to the next nerve cell in the circuit, telling it to conduct the impulse farther, or to stop.

Scientists have studied the neurotransmitters with the hope that knowledge of the chemistry underlying the transfer of information from one neuron to another will shed light on the larger problems of brain organization and function. Until a few years ago only a few chemicals were known to function as neurotransmitters. Adrenalin (or its close relative, noradrenalin) and acetylcholine were the earliest to be recognized. Beginning in the early 1970s, a whole series of new discoveries added several dozen new compounds to the list. Many of these are single amino acids. Some are small chains of amino acids, called peptides. No one can predict how many more will be found, as new discoveries are announced frequently.

And here is where the "convergence" problem arises again. Although thousands of compounds *could* serve as neurotransmitters, only a few dozen have been discovered to actually function as such. But when we look at a number of animals in different phyla, knowing that their brains evolved completely independently, we find the *same* set of compounds. This did not present a problem when there were only two or three identified neurotransmitters. One could easily postulate that some property of these specific molecules made them especially suitable for a neurotransmitter function even though we did not know what the specific property might be. Now, however, it appears extremely unlikely that a basic chemical property, so far unexplained, separates the eight or ten amino acids that have neurotransmitter activity from all the others that definitely do not. And it is even less likely that among the millions of small peptide molecules that cells are theoretically capable of making, the same few should be used again and again throughout the animal kingdom.

The reason that such consistency of substances functioning as neurotransmitters among different animal species presents a problem lies in the nature of neurotransmitter action. The response of the post-synaptic neuron does not depend on any particular chemical property of the transmitter molecule itself, but rather on the properties of the much larger molecules, called receptors, that are embedded in the membrane of the post-synaptic neuron itself. When the transmitter molecule lands on the receptor, it triggers a chemical reaction resulting in a change in the electric charge across the membrane. That, in turn, may cause either a new action potential to be generated, or it may make the post-synaptic neuron temporarily unable to generate a potential. The transmitter may be envisioned as a passive key, and the receptor molecule as the lock. It is not the shape of the key that determines what will be revealed when you unlock a door, it is what the lock is designed to secure. The same neurotransmitter molecule can act as a stimulating agent in one synapse, and as an inhibitor in another. The difference lies in the activity of the receptor, not in the properties of the transmitter.

Few biologists believe that the coincidental distribution of neurotransmitters among the various animal species reflects the paucity of suitable transmitter compounds. Nor is it seriously proposed that the rudimentary organisms that were ancestral to both the mollusks and the vertebrates, for instance, had any nervous system at all, much less one with the rich variety of neurotransmitters found in both the octopus and the rat. So the similarity cannot be explained as a common heritage from an early evolutionary stage.

It would take us too far from the subject of this book to pursue this question much further, but I do want to suggest that the beginning of a solution to the puzzle is in some ideas current among biologists. Living cells do often behave in ways that appear to indicate "planning." *The Selfish Gene*, a book by Richard Dawkins, presents a possibly overstated expression of these ideas.[7] The argument is too undeveloped to be called a theory, but if we had to give it a name, we might call it "biochemical teleology." Teleology, as we have seen, is the belief that nature is orderly because of the guidance and intervention of a deity. Much of the controversy over Darwin's theory was due to disagreement about the source of the manifest adaptiveness of many biological structures. Evolutionists argued with the teleologists, who claimed that God had created every living thing with a specific purpose and with deliberately designed adaptations for the fulfillment of that purpose. Biologists prefer to find general laws, such as adaptation and selection, rather than divine intervention, to "explain" biological functions. Thus teleology is regarded by most biologists as an unnecessary assumption. Nevertheless, it is obvious that living things do often behave in logical ways. Growth and development of a multicellular organism is clearly controlled and directed, so that, for example, the limb bud on a human embryo forms furrows and then divides itself to make exactly five toes. Individual embryonic cells must communicate among one another to follow some master plan in their division and migration. By contrast, a tumor grows wildly and without regulation or order.

Beyond the fact that they are almost certainly biochemical, the mechanisms for the regulation of growth and form are not clearly understood. Nevertheless, few biologists would abandon a mechanistic view of the phenomena in favor of a teleological explanation. There doesn't seem to be an adequate word to suggest merely that things behave according to a plan without the implication of a Divine Planner that proper usage of the term *teleological* would require. Hence "biochemical teleology," which suggests that the aggregates of molecules that make up cells have subtle properties beyond their immediate metabolic functions, and that they do tend to direct the destiny of the organism in certain ways. This brief sketch should make it clear that the mechanism by which such actions occur is assumed to be in accord with the laws of nature, and that we are not imputing a "purpose" to inanimate molecules.

Since the biochemical properties of cells are, in general, both more primitive and more uniform than the structure of whole organisms, it seems possible that a chemical framework common to all living animal groups is responsible for organizing the pathways that evolution has followed, to an extent sufficient to account for many of the mysterious coincidences found.

A somewhat more explicit expression of this argument is found in the overlapping areas of evolutionary theory and developmental genetics. The idea that there are specific genes that control the pattern of development is a very old one that largely succumbed to the "new" genetics of the 1940s and 1950s, when George Beadle and others established the biochemical basis of gene action. The hypothesis that each gene controlled the synthesis of a single enzyme was such a powerful explanation of the mysteries of how genes worked that it tended to obscure the fact that genes also do other things besides direct the synthesis of proteins. Earlier geneticists had implicitly assumed that some genes controlled chemical functions, others directed the behavior of the cell, and still others were responsible for the form and structure. Recognition of the biochemical basis of all cellular activities led to an oversimplification of the genetic mechanisms. The cell became "nothing but a bag of enzymes." The pendulum has swung back, and we now recognize that a great many genes have the function of regulating and controlling the activities of other genes, and that, particularly in the complex multicellular animals, the control genes far outnumber the "structural" genes responsible for the synthesis of enzymes.

Developmental genetics deals with the way groups of genes control the pattern of activity of other genes, switching them on and off at precisely coordinated times to produce the appropriate structural and functional effects. We now know of several systems in which a single gene may regulate a whole sequence of events leading to such profound consequences as, for example, the production of a complete extra set of wings in a fruit fly. It is not hard to imagine that such genes may be responsible for some of the dramatic jumps in evolution. Such thinking is providing re-newed support for the long-held view that development and evolution are closely related. If there is a genetically deter-mined program for the development of an embryo, simple modifications of this program, as by the accidental mutation of a single gene, or transposition of a single chromosome segment, could explain the sudden and drastic evolutionary jumps that are so embarrassing to the gradualist theory.

By an extension of the "biochemical teleology" argu-ment one might suggest that just as embryonic cells follow a "plan" in their development, large systems of neurons can also influence their own development and organization to enhance their ability to operate logically and efficiently. A large body of experimental evidence strongly indicates this self-organizing property of neural networks. It can even be demonstrated in computers. The inherent tendency of neu-rons to make logically functioning interconnections provides a plausible explanation for many of the spectacular cases of convergent evolution found in the nervous systems of unre-lated species of animals, just as the recognition that there are common principles of organization that guide and direct the genetic machinery of every cell makes it easier to under-stand why the same solutions to other biological problems have evolved again and again in separate groups of organ-isms.

If this discussion sounds overly speculative and theo-retical, it is because so little concrete evidence is available for the actual history of brain evolution. Soft structures such as brains, hearts, and kidneys tend to decay without fossiliz-ing, so we cannot trace the actual changes that took place in animals now extinct. Brain evolution is easier to follow than that of the visceral organs, since the cranium is a fairly good indication of the size and shape of the brain it contains, but we still can't tell much about the internal organization of the brain from fossil skulls. Thus we are forced to rely on specu-lation and indirect evidence in attempting to reconstruct the sequence of brain development.

The usual way of learning about the more primitive vertebrate brains is to look at the brains of living animals

that are thought to be representative of an earlier evolutionary stage. Comparative anatomy has its drawbacks as evidence of evolutionary history, since any animal living today
obviously has just as long an evolutionary history as any
other. However, it appears to be true that many species have
remained relatively unchanged over very long spans of time,
while other, originally closely related, species have changed.
Thus it can be assumed that a modern shark will still show
much the same anatomy and physiology as the sharks that
lived in the Permian era, long before any mammals had appeared. Such assumptions are quite generally accepted,
sometimes uncritically, but mostly with caution.

Unfortunately we do not have any living representatives of the earliest vertebrate species. Thus we can only
guess at the structure of the most primitive vertebrate nervous system. All living vertebrates have a complex, highly
developed brain in which groups of neurons engaged in similar functions tend to clump together in gray "nuclei" surrounded by white matter. The white matter is composed of
the numerous fiber tracts that form a complex network interconnecting the cell bodies of the neurons.

In the primitive condition of the vertebrate brain, the
major concentration of cell bodies was always on the inside
of the neural mass, and the white fiber tracts formed an
outer layer. That primitive arrangement is still found in the
spinal cord of all vertebrates. In the brain, however, there
has been a progressive tendency for more and more cell
bodies to migrate to the outer layers, and so in the newer
parts of the brain, for instance the cerebral hemispheres, an
outer cortex of gray matter or cell bodies surrounds an inner
layer of white matter. Embedded in that inner white matter
are still found many clumps of gray matter—evidence of the
more primitive arrangement. Thus the most primitive vertebrates probably had a nervous system that was hardly more
than a spinal cord, and the thrust of evolution has resulted in
a greater and greater "cephalization" or increase in the concentration of neurons at the head end of the animal, followed
by an increase in the size and extent of the external gray cortex.

We can only speculate on the structures of the simpler stages of brain evolution that are missing from the fossil record. When we look for evidence from the study of living species, we attempt to reconstruct a phylogenetic sequence according to the overall body characteristics of the vertebrates. Among the most primitive vertebrates were the cyclostomes, which were jawless, boneless fish. A living representative of this class is the lamprey eel. The lamprey has a good set of sense organs and is an agile and powerful swimmer. Having no jaws, it attaches itself to the body of large fish by means of a sucker disk and rasps away the skin to feed on the soft tissues. The brain is not much differentiated from the spinal cord and can be considered as having two main divisions—a motor brain for controlling the musculature, to enable the lamprey to catch and attach itself to its prey, and a sensory brain for receiving information from the sense organs. (A third division is present in all vertebrates—the visceral brain. It controls the internal "housekeeping" functions of the body, such as breathing, heart rate, and digestion. We will not be considering that division.) So at the earliest level of vertebrate evolution for which we have living representatives we might consider the brain limited to a motor division and a sensory division, with, of course, reflex pathways connecting the input signals to the appropriate muscles for a response.

A major step in the early evolution of the vertebrates was the appearance of a lower jaw. If we take that development as an index of the next stage in our study of the brain, we can find a modern representative in the shark. The shark has a new addition besides the motor brain and the sensory brain: the thalamus. The thalamus apparently developed from the sensory brain, and it receives input from several different sense organs. It also has connections to the motor brain, and it processes information for some reflex activity. In addition to these motor and sensory functions, the thalamus is also the center for a "new" level of function that we call the affective brain. This is the part of the brain that generates the emotions. When we use the word *emotions* we generally think in terms of human emotions, and this would not be an appropriate description of what goes on in a shark's brain. Nevertheless, from their actions it is obvious that sharks do experience fear, rage, hunger, and sexual desire, and the "centers" for those feelings are in the thalamic region of the brain. So we can conclude that at the level of evolution that produced the elasmobranch (cartilaginous fishes) the affective brain was beginning to develop.

With the evolution of bone, the vertebrates reached the next stage of body form and structure. Modern bony fish have a somewhat more complex and generally larger brain than that of sharks of comparable size. Fish have the beginnings of a fairly distinct cerebrum, and this structure is associated with the cognitive faculties. Thus by the time a bony skeleton had evolved, the vertebrate brain already had all four of its modern components: the motor brain, the sensory brain, the affective brain, and the cognitive brain. Subsequent evolution, through the amphibians and reptiles and then into the birds and mammals, has been a continuation of the growth in size and complexity of these four divisions, although not in equal degrees.

Since neurons have the habit of migrating from place to place, the exact location of many structures in the vertebrate nervous system has changed during the course of evolution. A similar shift of location often occurs during the embryonic development of the brain. It is somewhat easier to work backwards, both in evolution and in embryology. Once a structure has developed fully and can be observed in its final functional form, it is possible to see more clearly in retrospect what the poorly defined and relatively undifferentiated group of nerve cells was destined to become. Also, knowing what to look for, we can sometimes trace the form and function of a neural structure even before it has realized its full potential. We should remember that evolutionary selection can operate only on what *is*, never on what might be. New structures cannot be assembled on hope, but only by improvements and embellishments on an operating system. Thus, for example, before the thalamus became a recognizable structure, there must have been some precursor, which had to be functional, rather than inchoate. We can hardly imagine what sort of emotional life a lamprey experiences, but the lack of a clearly differentiated set of subthalamic nuclei that, in later forms, became the center for "drives" should not lead us to the conclusion that emotions were brand-new inventions of the shark, and that more primitive vertebrates entirely lacked an affective brain.

It is difficult to avoid a kind of biological chauvinism when talking about brain evolution. The vertebrates do certainly have a very complex and excellent brain. Among the vertebrates, the mammals have reached the highest level of brain size and specialization. And among the mammals, humans are obviously the best! Therefore it is tempting to regard brain evolution as an arrow leading from the lowliest forms straight to us. Evolutionary changes that seem to favor human kinds of brain development are "good," whereas other kinds of brain specializations are "dead ends."

Biologists should make every effort to avoid such chauvinistic attitudes; but specialists in invertebrate biology will testify that the effort is frequently unsuccessful. Perhaps if we understood more about insects' brains, or their mental life, we would be less parochial in our outlook. But as it is, we tend to think of the human brain as the Platonic ideal toward which Nature has been striving through the long course of evolutionary history, and all other models as imperfect experiments that fell short of their goal. (The irony of this passage is not intended to be heavy-handed. I have not escaped this chauvinism. I really do believe that my brain is better than that of an octopus. But I recognize that that is because my brain is called upon to do things that make sense for a human. If I had to live the life of an octopus, my view might be that an octopus brain would serve me better.)

Granting that our discussion is limited to the evolutionary history of vertebrate brains only, we can find some general principles that seem to justify a kind of hierarchy of development leading straight toward us. The basic rule seems to be that certain functions are improved by adding more and more circuitry (neurons) up to some limit, and then a new start is made with a whole new structure. However, evolution has other rules that must also be obeyed. One cardinal principle is that you can never shut down for alterations. Every new development must be acquired in such a manner as to permit the older structures to continue to operate. As a result, the new structures never really replace the old, but simply add on, integrating their activities with the simpler, more primitive mechanisms that were there first. T. S. Eliot, in the lines from *Four Quartets* quoted at the beginning of this chapter, warns about "superficial notions of evolution" that lead the "popular mind" to denigrate the past. We could not enjoy the richness of our human brain if it did not also include the brain of a reptile, a shark, and even a lamprey. We can still find all the features of the shark's brain in our own. Both structurally and functionally, our brains have everything the shark has, plus much that has been added on since. It was not just a metaphor when Martin Luther spoke of "putting down the *old man!*" He meant the unredeemed sinner, before salvation, but in a less theological sense the old man is still with us. Our brutish ancestors are there in our brains, ready to erupt at any strong incitement, or when our newer, more sensitive circuits are inhibited by fatigue or alcohol. Fortunately those primitive drives are usually held in check by an overlay of finer sensibilities. We have an intellect that appreciates the strategic advantage of being able to smile and wait when an offense is given, instead of attacking immediately, like an animal.

The structure and organization of the human brain nicely illustrate the principle of adding new parts to old. We are certainly not descended from turtles, but the humble turtle, though a very specialized animal, has a brain reasonably representative of the reptilian level of vertebrate evolution. As mammals descended from reptiles, it seems reasonable to compare the brain of a modern turtle with that of a human to see how far we have come. As illustrated in Figure 17, the turtle brain has all of the basic structures found in the human brain. The most outstanding anatomical differences are the

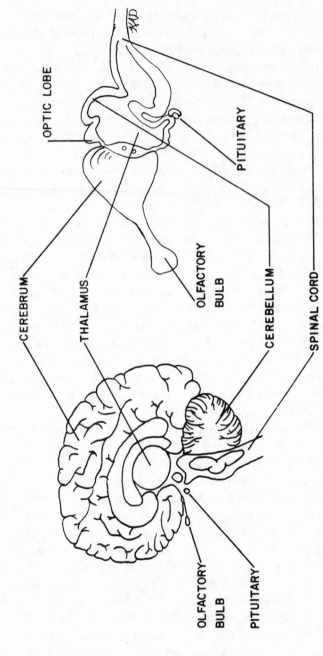

Figure 17. Comparison of a human brain with that of a turtle.

vast increase in size and complexity of the cerebrum and cerebellum of the human brain. But functional changes are even more profound. The differences will be clearer if we take them up under the four general categories of brain function: motor, sensory, affective, and cognitive.

The most elementary level of the motor brain consists of the reflex control centers in the spinal cord and in the brain stem. Those centers are more or less equivalent in both human and turtle nervous systems. A painful stimulus to the foot will cause a sharp withdrawal reaction in either animal, and the spinal cord has all the necessary circuitry to accomplish the movement, without any help from the brain. A second and higher level of integration and coordination is carried out in the cerebellum, which is much larger and more elaborate in mammals than in reptiles. Lewis Carroll's turtle studied reeling, writhing, and fainting in coils in school. He would never have been able to master writing, even if the linguistic capability had existed in his brain. Not only do turtles lack flexible fingers, but they do not have the complex cerebellar coordination that would be required to manipulate a pencil.

Finally, a third level of motor control evolved in the cerebrum, and in humans the whole posterior margin of the frontal lobe of the cerebrum is concerned with voluntary movements. Each level acts through the lower and more primitive levels, adding on to, but never replacing, what was there before. A nice example of this can be seen in the regulation of the facial muscles. Norman Geschwind tells of a brain-injured patient who was unable to control his muscles to produce a smile on command, but who smiled normally when told a joke.[8] The cerebrum controls the muscles by direct circuits activated by the conscious "will," but other, more primitive pathways, which were uninjured in that patient, can also take command when an emotional impulse calls for a smile. A neurologist might describe classical acting technique as a studied activation of the facial musculature in order to simulate, by direct cerebral control, the expressions appropriate to the character being depicted. The

"Method" actor, on the other hand, bypasses the conscious level and attempts to create the appropriate facial movements automatically, by generating the emotions appropriate to the part being played.

The sensory brain, too, has increased both its size and its complexity, and again, large areas of the cerebrum have sensory functions that in more primitive nervous systems are carried on at a simpler level by primary sensory neurons and lower levels of the brain and spinal cord. In the turtle, for example, a pair of large lumps called the optic lobes project from the brainstem (see Figure 18). They receive the information carried by the optic nerves and are the turtle's main center for processing visual information. We have the same structures, but they are not as obvious, for the brain stem has swelled around them, so they no longer project from the surface. Even if they did, they would be hidden under the vastly expanded cerebral lobes. In the human brain we don't even call them optic lobes. They still receive the optic nerves and serve as processors of visual information, but we now consider them an intermediate station of the visual pathway and call them a part of the thalamic nucleus. Our cerebrum has taken over the higher levels of visual interpretation—the conscious interpretation of the meanings of visual patterns—and the whole occipital lobe of the cerebral hemispheres is engaged in that activity. "Taken over" is perhaps misleading if it implies that what our occipital lobe does for us, the optic lobe does for the turtle. The closest thing we have to an optic lobe is the optic nucleus of

Figure 18.

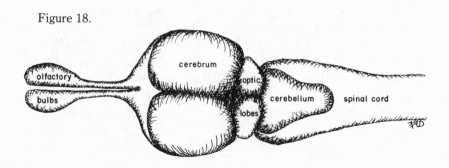

olfactory

bulbs

cerebrum

optic

lobes

cerebellum

spinal cord

our thalamus. The turtle doesn't really have anything to correspond to the vast processing areas of our visual cortex of the cerebrum. Alice's poor mock turtle could not have studied reading either, for again, regardless of the problem of a linguistic capacity, he would not have sufficient visual processing power to discriminate even the letters of the alphabet. Turtles simply do not possess the kind of complex integration and interpretation that makes vision so rich and informative for humans.

The turtle's affective brain is limited to a few clusters of neurons in and underneath the thalamus. In the human a whole complex called the limbic system has developed, forming a sort of ring around the thalamus. The complexity and pervasive influence of this emotion-generating system in humans are staggering. Like the motor and sensory brains, the affective brain has also invaded the enlarging cerebrum, and the relationship between our "feelings" (affective brain) and our "thoughts" (cognitive brain) is so intimate that we should not expect any great anatomical separation of the two kinds of cerebral activity. Feelings, like memory, cannot be localized to any particular portion of the cerebral cortex.

We are well aware of the pervasive influence of our affective brain. Humans are certainly as much *Homo affectans* as we are *Homo sapiens*; as much feeling as thinking creatures. Miguel de Unamuno, writing in 1921, put it well:

> Man is said to be a reasoning animal. I do not
> know why he has not been defined as an affective
> or feeling animal. Perhaps that which differenti-
> ates him from other animals is feeling rather than
> reason. More often I have seen a cat reason than
> laugh or weep. Perhaps it weeps or laughs in-
> wardly—but then perhaps, also inwardly, the crab
> resolves equations of the second degree.[9]

It is unlikely that Unamuno would deny feelings to animals. Obviously emotions are not peculiar to humans. What is unique is the combination of the affective and the cognitive mind that makes us aware of the emotional richness of our lives. Emotion without consciousness is like a dog yelping in his sleep, or the reflex cry of an anaesthetized patient. There is activity in the nervous system, but it is not being experienced. A tree falling in the forest really falls, whether or not anyone is there to see or hear, but pain or sadness can have no real existence unless they are perceived.

Perception brings us to the cognitive brain itself, associated anatomically with the cortex of gray matter that makes up the outer layer of the cerebral hemispheres. In the human brain the cortical region has outgrown all other parts of the brain to such a degree that it forces the cerebrum into a mass of complex folds. In Figure 19 the differences between the human brain and those of other vertebrates can be seen. The two halves of the human cerebrum almost completely cover all but the hindmost parts of the rest of the brain. By contrast, the cerebrum of the turtle is an unimpressive little bump on the forebrain, quite overshadowed by the olfactory lobes. We cannot deny the turtle some level of cognition. What level, however, is difficult to judge. Our vocabulary is too anthropocentric to be very useful in describing the states of consciousness of nonhumans. "Cognition" has a certain meaning to humans, and it is intuitively inseparable from the kind of consciousness that we humans enjoy. None of us has ever been a turtle, so we cannot know what sort of sentience the lower vertebrates experience. All we can say is that the turtle seems to be aware of his surroundings, he reacts more or less sensibly to new situations, and he shows a modest ability to learn and to remember. These functions we believe to be localized in his cerebrum. The intellectual difference between a turtle and a human child is not inconsistent with the difference in size and complexity of their respective cerebrums. In anatomical terms, a human fetus surpasses a turtle about four weeks after conception.

Despite the reservations expressed earlier about assuming an evolutionary sequence on the basis of comparisons with modern species of different levels of "primitiveness," a set of brains from different animals could be assembled to show a most convincing and orderly progres-

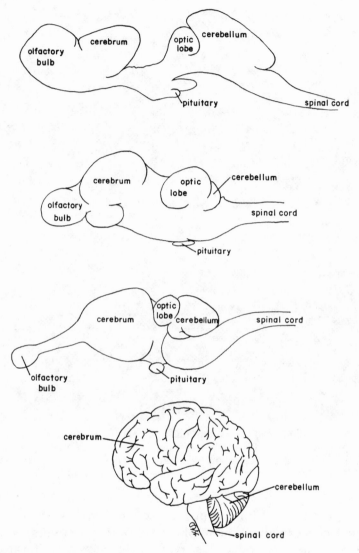

Figure 19. Evolution of the vertebrate brain. From the top: shark, frog, alligator, human.

sion from the lamprey through the human (see Figure 20). In fact, neuroscientists are accustomed to assuming the regularity of the evolutionary relationships in living species and often plan experiments utilizing whatever animal seems

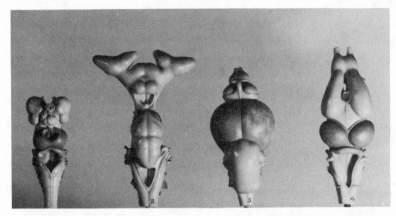

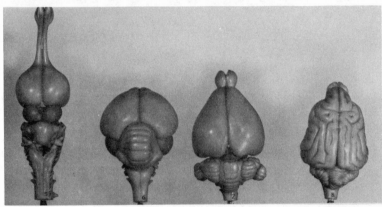

Figure 20. Photographs of anatomical models of vertebrate brains: (1) a lamprey, (2) a shark, (3) a fish, (4) an amphibian, (5) a reptile, (6) a bird, (7) a rabbit, and (8) a carnivore. The models are not made to the same scale.

most convenient for the procedure employed, with not too much concern about the implications of their findings for human nervous systems. A survey of the scientific literature would lead one to conclude that scientists had an extraordinary interest in rats, unless it was recognized that rats are generally regarded as cheap but valid models for biological processes that are relevant to higher animals. It is reasonable to believe that most of the basic physiological mechanisms that govern neuronal interactions are consistent whether we look at the brain of a frog, a rat, or a human. Where experimenters have been criticized for using lower animals it has usually been because the particular mechanisms they were studying were too complex to be fully developed in animals of that level of brain development. The way a rat learns to find his way through a maze is a very poor model for the way a human child learns to read.

An alternative search for the evolutionary history of the brain avoids some of the problems inherent in using various species of animals with different evolutionary adaptations. The approach is based on the relationship between the embryonic development of the individual and its phylogenetic past. Although sometimes misunderstood, the recognition that each individual, in its development, goes through a morphological sequence analogous to the evolutionary pattern of its phylum is valid enough to provide evidence about our ancestors. The most familiar example is the gill slits that appear at a certain stage of the mammalian embryo, only to be reworked into jaw and throat structures at a later stage of development. Another is the tail that grows on early human embryos, but which does not persist in later stages. This principle has been summarized in the slogan "ontogeny recapitulates phylogeny."

Embryonic gills and tails are an interesting reminder of our common evolutionary past, but we can observe a rather more spectacular example of the reordering of the body in those animals that undergo metamorphosis. The evolutionary history of the organism may be "recapitulated" in metamorphosis, just as it is in embryonic development. The rule must be applied with caution. It is not literally true that a caterpillar is more primitive than a butterfly, but a worm-like body plan is certainly less specialized than that of the flying insect.

Metamorphosis is rare in the vertebrates. The most familiar case is the change from a tadpole to a frog or salamander. It is an oversimplification to suggest that the development from a tadpole to a frog exactly recapitulates the evolution of amphibians from fish, but the shift from a water-living animal with gills to an air-breathing form with legs and arms requires a series of changes that are remarkably similar, whether they take place in one individual in a few weeks, or in thousands of generations over geologic ages.

One particular example of such changes is of special interest, since it involves the nervous system directly. In the tadpole, as in fish, a lateral line sense organ runs along each side of the body. As the tadpole metamorphoses into a frog, many of the sensory receptors and the nerves carrying their messages to the brain migrate from the lateral line and cluster into a new location in the neck region. The new structure is a cochlea, the tiny coiled organ of the inner ear that receives the vibrations from our eardrums and converts them into a neural code for loudness and pitch of sound. Thus the organ that sensed pressure waves under water "evolves" into an organ for receiving sound waves in air. In an almost literal sense, the tadpole recapitulates in a few weeks the changes that evolved over millions of years in the development of a hearing organ for land animals.

Looking at the embryonic growth of the human brain, we see a pattern of development that does indeed recapitulate, to a remarkable degree, the evolutionary history of our species. This sequence continues through post-natal development, but we must be very cautious in taking the relationships between developmental and evolutionary stages literally. The principle has often been abused. A human child at the pre-linguistic stage of its development is *not* a chimpanzee, no matter how persuasive the similarities may be. The embryos of apes and humans show a very similar pattern of neurological structures until the later stages. However, the final forms of each species reflect the specific adaptations in the evolutionary history of both humans and apes in the time since their ancestors diverged from a common population several million years ago. Neither the ape nor the turtle remains in a neurological state like that of an early human embryo.

Putting together what we know, both from comparative studies of other vertebrates and from brain development in humans, we can trace a reasonable pattern for the probable evolutionary history of our brain up to the final jump into linguistic competence. That final step itself cannot be observed in lower animals, since they do not attain it. Human embryology does not give much help either, partly because much of the final development with which we are concerned occurs post-natally, and also because the ultimate step, though profound, is not reflected in gross anatomical changes so much as in a subtle reorganization of the fine structure of the neural circuits.

At this point we must retreat somewhat from the emphasis on conservatism in brain evolution. While it is true that "new" structures preserve the earlier adaptations, it is also possible for very dramatic remodeling to take place. The brain is by far the most plastic organ of the body, and drastic reorganization can occur within relatively few generations. Imagine the extent of the changes required to go from the two separate visual processing centers found in most animals to a binocular vision system. Where a sheep or a turtle sees an almost completely separate scene with each eye, humans have both eyes aimed at the same point and see one integrated "seamless" panorama. One would think that reorganizing the visual fields would require very substantial rewiring of the neural circuits, along with large changes in the gross morphology of the brain. And yet we find, both among the birds and the mammals, many species with monocular vision, and some with binocular vision, and the neurological differences are so subtle that it is sometimes hard to determine, from anatomical observations, which is which.

The evolutionary developments that led to the large-scale lateral specialization of the two cerebral hemispheres, although drastic in their effect, were like the example of binocular vision in that they did not require any conspicuous anatomical changes. Lateral specialization of the cerebrum is probably essential for consciousness, but once again we are faced with the difficulty discussed in Chapter One—we cannot trace the evolution of bilateral specialization by examination of fossils because the changes are not visible in gross anatomical terms. Comparative studies are of little use, since lower animals have not evolved lateral specialization in the sense humans did. Cultural evidence from the time of the transition is sparse and difficult to interpret. Stone tools from early Neanderthal sites have not shown any evidence of a right-hand preference, so one might conclude that the motor dominance that accompanied the lateralization of the cerebral hemispheres came suddenly, at about the time language itself appeared.

If we cannot trace the evolution of lateral specialization in humans, we can at least describe what it has led to. Most of the evidence is recent, largely derived from a small number of epilepsy patients who have undergone surgical severing of the corpus callosum, the huge band of fiber tracts that connect the right and left side of the brain, both anatomically and functionally. One might reasonably expect that such an operation would leave the patients so crippled neurologically that they could hardly function at all. Instead, surprisingly, several of them appear to be quite normal in every function that can be observed casually. (Some of the patients had severe brain damage associated with the epilepsy that the operation was undertaken to control, and these cases cannot be studied with much confidence.) Two rather spectacular principles emerged from the scientific study of these patients. One is that a number of high-level intellectual functions appear to be localized in the right or the left cerebral hemisphere. Besides language itself, these include logical, analytical, and mathematical functions in the left hemisphere and artistic and geometric skills in the right. The second principle is that when these hemispheres are separated surgically, each half seems to display a kind of independent consciousness, so when we communicate with the half that retains control of the speech apparatus, we are talking to only one set of the traits that, in the pre-operated patient, were completely integrated into a single personality. When we manage to communicate with the "silent" hemisphere, we discover that it too has a consciousness and a set of characteristics that complement rather than duplicate those of the speaking hemisphere.

After the publication of the studies of Roger Sperry and his colleagues at The California Institute of Technology, interest in the study of commissurotomy patients expanded rapidly, with a great deal of publicity given to the early findings. Many of the general public and some popular writers misunderstood the implications of the reports. Since the lateral specialization is so crucial to both language and consciousness, it is important to correct some of the false impressions about the organization of the conscious functions in the two halves of the cerebrum.

1. We do *not* have two brains. In the normal individual, the millions and millions of fibers that make up the corpus callosum permit perfect and instantaneous communication between the right and left hemisphere and complete integration of their various functional areas. Only in the extremely abnormal condition of artificial severance of these lines of communication do the two halves appear to develop an independence from each other.

2. One hemisphere is not "dominant" over the other. For every function that shows such a pattern of lateral localization, one hemisphere is more specialized than the other and consequently "better" at it. The "good" side appears to suppress the corresponding part of the "poorer" side. However, the specializations are distributed to both halves of the cerebrum, and neither side is better at everything. Nor is the suppressed region completely lacking in the ability that is normally carried out by the opposite hemisphere. This accounts for the common observation that functions lost through unilateral brain damage are often regained by "reeducation" of the formerly inhibited intact hemisphere. Thus dominance is not a property of a whole cerebral hemisphere, but only of a specific localized region; it is usually not absolute; and while the corpus callosum is intact, it is undetectable, and consequently largely irrelevant.

3. Language is not limited to one hemisphere. Memory is involved in the storage of vocabulary, and memory is

stored holographically on both sides of the cerebrum. The retrieval of the stored symbols that make up language, and the syntactic rules that organize those symbols into meaningful combinations, are the functions of the so-called language areas of the brain, and these areas are normally found only in one hemisphere. However, the functions performed by the language area are not unique, and the other hemisphere can take up the function after the primary language area has been destroyed by injury or disease. In patients with a severed corpus callosum, the "silent" hemisphere can be shown to have language, and even the power to read and write, albeit rather poorly. The recent evidence suggests that the language abilities of the non–language hemisphere are greatly enhanced when there has been long-standing damage to the language hemisphere. This indicates that the language abilities of the brain are bilateral, but that one hemisphere normally takes on the function and inhibits the development of the other. After the release from inhibition, language functions take time to develop, and it is possible that older brains are unable to learn language very well for reasons unrelated to inhibition, as we observe in normal humans attempting to learn new languages late in life.

4. The consciousness of the hemisphere that retains access to the speech apparatus is not altered in any very obvious way by its severance from the other half, although many mental abilities that depend on the specializations of the detached hemisphere are missing, or at least profoundly impaired. This is a very curious matter, and there is little agreement about the question of where the consciousness resides, or whether the split-brain patients have one consciousness or two. Michael Gazzaniga comments on the mysterious absence of recognition by the speaking hemisphere that its other hemisphere is missing, after commissurotomy. He says, "Indeed, one would miss the departure of a good friend more, apparently, than the left hemisphere misses the right."[10] The problem is made more difficult by the extreme difficulty in communicating with the non-lan-

guage hemisphere, to ask it for its introspective rumina-
tions. Whatever the case, it is well to emphasize again point
1. Unless you have had your corpus callosum severed, you
do *not* have two different consciousnesses, or two different
personalities, speaking to each other across the longitudinal
fissure. The intact brain is a single entity. Both hemispheres
are you.

Although lateral differentiation has occurred in
many brain functions at a more primitive level than those
discussed in this chapter, the degree of cerebral differentiation of all nonhuman animals is so much less than ours that
specialization of cognitive and symbolic functions on a
right–left pattern appears to be a uniquely human attribute.
It is clear that such lateral specialization is intimately related
to the development of language, and equally with consciousness. Beyond that we cannot trace the exact relationship.
Perhaps with the continuation of the fascinating studies of
split-brain patients we shall learn more about the anatomical
localization of the higher cerebral functions.

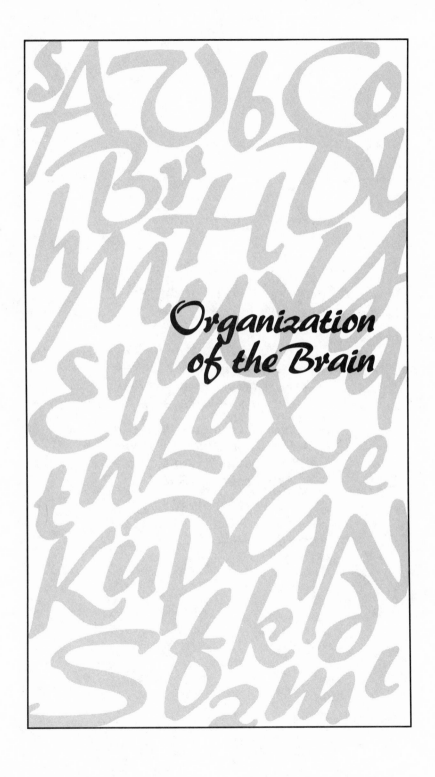

Organization of the Brain

The Brain—is wider than the Sky—
For—put them side by side—
The one the other will contain
With ease—and You—beside—

The Brain is deeper than the sea—
For—hold them—Blue to Blue—
The one the other will absorb—
As Sponges—buckets—do—

The Brain is just the weight of God—
For—Heft them—Pound for Pound—
And they will differ—if they do—
As Syllable from Sound—

EMILY DICKINSON[11]

NINETEENTH-CENTURY ENGLISH boarding schools taught "reading and writing and painting in oils," none of which could have been mastered by Lewis Carroll's mock turtle. Most other mental functions that humans have and lower vertebrates lack involve language, either directly or indirectly, and along with language itself depend on two special adaptations of the human brain. The first is the differentiation of function between the right and left halves of the cerebrum, as described in the previous chapter. The second is a form of information processing that, in the absence of a better term, we call holographic.

Holographic processing is hard to describe because we have very little understanding of how it really works. The term is loosely used by many neuroscientists, chiefly those who study the physiological mechanisms of memory. Its meaning derives from laser photographs, called holograms, in which the pictorial information is stored diffusely in the emulsion of the film, rather than in specific locations for each part of the picture, as in a conventional photographic negative. To view the laser hologram, the information must be gathered from the whole—that is, the picture is restored holistically, rather than piece by piece. Human memories are stored in the brain in an analogous fashion, with no particular area devoted to any special class of memory, but rather with the whole cortex working holistically to store and retrieve the information. Of course we have very little real knowledge of memory mechanisms, so memory specialists are unable to tell us very much about holographic processes in the brain. What they have made clear is that there are two aspects of memory research. One is a study of how memories are stored, and the other is the search for the mechanisms by which the stored memories are retrieved. By now it is clear to almost everyone that the storage of memories is holographic. It is not as universally recognized that the retrieval also involves holographic processing.

Memory is of fundamental importance to humans. The sum of our individual memories constitutes most of our idea of self. Our futures are veiled. The present is only an ever-changing instant in time. It is our past that makes each of us what we are, and the past, though it may be retained in the form of scars or possessions, affects us primarily through our memory. But memories stored are of no more use than gold hoarded in a vault. Their real value can be realized only when they are used; and for memory, use means retrieval—finding the memory and making it once again a present experience by bringing it into consciousness. The retrieval process brings us closest to the subject of consciousness, for experiencing that which is dredged from our memory and experiencing events that are happening in the present instant are both manifestations of the same stream of consciousness, which, in its fullest meaning, is a uniquely human capability. Recognition that an understanding of memory requires an understanding of consciousness brings us full circle: To understand memory we must understand consciousness, and to understand consciousness we should look at memory.

When we say that memory storage is holographic, we mean that it has certain characteristics that are identifiable in other kinds of holographic processes. We don't know enough about the ways the brain processes information to describe the mechanism, but we can use the photographic hologram as an analogy. Even this modest effort to explain the term is not easy, since the basic principles of holography are not well understood. However, hologram pictures are familiar enough to provide us with a starting place.

To make a hologram one places an unexposed film in front of the object to be photographed and illuminates both the film and the object with a beam of coherent light (all the waves are in phase with one another) from a laser. Laser light is also monochromatic—that is, of one color. Color is determined by the wavelength of light, and since wavelength varies with the frequency of the light, the laser output waves could not be in phase unless they were all of the same length. No lens is used to focus the scene on the film. The direct light from the laser and the light scattered by the object both fall on the film. However, the scattered light has traveled a slightly different distance from the source and consequently has its phase shifted from that of the direct beam. Any given spot on the film receives light in a variety of different phase relationships from all parts of the illuminated object. The grains of silver simply respond to the total amount of light, and since rays that are in phase add, and rays that are out of phase cancel one another, the developed film will be a record of the total set of phase relationships that existed on each part of the negative (see Figure 21).

When you look at a hologram of, say, a model airplane, all you see is a somewhat fogged film, with no indication of a picture. Nevertheless, encoded in the pattern of the reduced silver grains is all the information about the phase relationships of the light reflected from the model, and those phase relationships in turn encode the information about the shape of the wings, the fuselage, and the propeller. To "decode" the picture, all that is needed is to shine light of approximately the same wavelength as the original laser beam (it need not be coherent) through the negative. If you look through the negative at the colored light, you find that the silver grains interfere with its passage in such a way as to mimic the original relationships of the laser beam reflected by the toy. You see a phantom airplane floating in space at

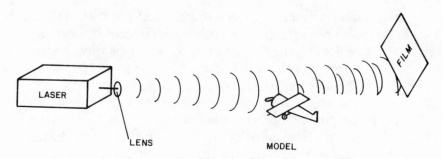

Figure 21. Laser holography. The laser beam, spread out by means of a lens, illuminates both the film and the object being photographed. Light deflected by the model reaches the film out of phase with the undeflected beam. The phase differences result in addition or cancellation of the light waves, thereby producing a pattern of intensity on the sensitive film that, after development, can be used to recreate the original scene.

the same distance from the film as the real model was at the time of the exposure. The picture is not "on" the film, as an ordinary picture would be, but behind the film. Indeed, if you focus your eyes on the film, the picture will be out of focus. To see it clearly, you must focus on the spot where the image appears. Thus the pattern of silver grains in the emulsion is not the picture itself, but a mechanism that acts on the transmitted light in such a way as to recreate the scene.

What are the characteristics of a hologram that make it a useful analogy for holographic information processing in memory? First, there are two processes: storage and retrieval. The scene was stored in the photographic emulsion at the time the picture was taken, but it cannot be viewed without a certain retrieval procedure. Already we can see the analogy with mental function. Memory also requires separate processes for storage and for retrieval. And this is true not only of memory but of consciousness as well. One might consider all of the consciousness that we humans enjoy as a complex system of orderly retrieval of stored symbols that not only provide us with a code for language but make up the very substance of our mental experience.

The identification of consciousness with the retrieval of holographically stored symbolic information points to the relationship between language and memory. Wordsworth described a scene encountered on a walk:

> . . . I saw a crowd,
> A host, of golden daffodils;
> Beside the lake, beneath the trees,
> Fluttering and dancing in the breeze.

Later he wrote of retrieving the vision from his memory. Anyone remembering the poem can, through retrieval of the verbal symbols, recreate the same scene that the poet had stored visually. It hardly matters whether Wordsworth ever actually saw those daffodils. His consciousness could have made up the whole scene. The important thing is that by translating his inner experience, whether imagined or real, into verbal symbols, he made that vision a precious memory for generations of readers, a memory of a meadow of daffodils we never actually beheld. But for all of us,

> They flash upon that inward eye
> Which is the bliss of solitude.

Another characteristic of a hologram is that, unlike an ordinary photograph, it stores the information about every part of the scene in every part of the negative. If you cut out a small piece of an ordinary negative taken with a camera, you will have all the information about one small portion of the picture in that piece, perhaps the tip of one wing of our airplane model. The remainder of the negative will show all the rest of the plane, but it will tell you nothing at all about the missing wingtip. If, on the other hand, you were to cut out a portion of a hologram, the small piece you cut out still gives you the whole scene, albeit with somewhat less clarity and detail. Likewise the remainder of the negative is not missing any part of the original plane: the wings, tail, and fuselage—all are there. There would be a hole in the negative, but the picture you reconstruct by looking through any portion remaining would be complete. Also, since each part of the negative has "the whole picture" in it, you will see the original scene in three dimensions, and by moving your viewpoint you can see part way around the image.

Holographic storage, then, has the very special property that the information is stored "everywhere." This is one of the most startling correspondences between the hologram and human memory. Our memories are likewise stored "everywhere" in our brain. There is no part of the cerebrum you could cut out and thereby destroy the specific memory of, say, your grandfather's face. Each part of your cerebral cortex, astonishingly, contains the entire rich store of all your memories. Gross injuries to the cerebrum may be sustained with no observable loss of any specific set of memories, and in the history of clinical observation, such injuries have been observed in every part of the brain.

Of course there is a limit to the amount of tissue you can remove and still have memory, just as there is a minimum size of a hologram that will reconstruct the image. However, long before you reach the minimum of brain needed for storage, you will have lost the functional integrity needed for retrieval, so the storage problem becomes moot.

In human memory the retrieval mechanism is much more complex and sensitive than the storage system, so we often encounter difficulties in retrieval, even though the memories are still intact. We have all struggled to recall a name, a line of poetry, or where we left a key. Later, perhaps after the need has passed, the memory springs unbidden to our consciousness. Clearly it has been there all the time, hidden somewhere in the dark recesses of our mind, but—at least temporarily—inaccessible. A blow to the head, poisoning, anoxia, severe illness, or even an emotional shock can disable the retrieval system. Amnesias are defects in the retrieval system, not actual loss of the memories themselves. This becomes obvious when, as frequently happens, amnesiacs recover. Recovery may be slow or dramatically fast, but in either case, the "lost" memories do not have to be relearned. They were there all the time, but simply irretrievable.

Similarly for the special part of memory that stores the vocabulary, there is no particular place in the brain where words are hoarded. The "language areas" of the brain are the regions where the rules of syntax are used to direct the retrieval and processing of the language symbols, not a place where they are stored. As with other kinds of amnesias, when brain injury produces aphasia, the actual memory of the words is not impaired, just the ability to retrieve them. Again, when aphasics recover—as they often do—the words do not have to be relearned. They were there all along, but inaccessible; locked up.

So the brain is like an enormous hologram. All of the neural symbols used for language, visual memories, music, feelings, are stored "everywhere," and the phenomenon we call "consciousness" consists of a process of orderly retrieval and organization of these symbols to produce sentences, scenes, and meanings of every kind. R. W. Girard once described memory as a vast dark warehouse, filled with a multitude of objects. Retrieval is you with a flashlight. You can shine your light here or there and see parts of the contents, but never more than a tiny fraction at one time.

Unfortunately the actual form of memory storage is not yet known. The unit of memory has been called the "engram." The search for the engram has occupied neuroscientists for many years, but much of that effort has been wasted because of the failure to appreciate the quality of holographic storage. When we think of memory as a "thing"—a particular synaptic configuration, a complex molecule, whatever—we naturally think of it as being localized in a certain spot in the brain. Recognition that memories are stored diffusely, "everywhere," points up the hopelessness of looking for a particular RNA molecule, for instance, that encodes the memory of your grandfather's face.

If the holographic storage of neural information is difficult to understand, the other half of the problem, the retrieval of that information, is infinitely harder. Basically we know nothing whatsoever about it. We are only beginning to understand the mechanisms of photographic holograms, and that knowledge would provide, at best, a mere analogy for the much more complex problem of neural processing.

Perhaps the best we can do is to point out some of the probable features of the mental processes that shine the light on some of the contents of that dark warehouse which is memory and make a few predictions about future discoveries in this field.

One way of getting at the problem is to recognize more explicitly that when we talk about memory retrieval we are talking about consciousness. Retrieval of a memory means precisely that we are bringing it into our consciousness. It is but a small step to say that retrieval *is* consciousness, and when we recognize the intimate relationship between consciousness and language, all three come into a sharper focus. All involve the special intermodal processing that utilizes symbols that stand for real things, rather than simply sensory messages *about* things. Language itself is both a tool for memory retrieval and a special form *of* memory retrieval—the retrieval of the particular symbols that make up our language, following the syntactic rules that organize those symbols into meaning.

It follows that memory retrieval in lower animals, lacking language, must be a very different phenomenon, and that is true. Much of the confusion in research about the mechanisms of memory has resulted from a failure to recognize the distinctions between conscious recollection in humans and the much simpler kind of memory, which we share with lower animals—that involved in learning a motor skill, finding the way home, and recognizing that the sound of the refrigerator door may be a signal for food. Rats and pigeons are good experimental subjects for studies on the neural mechanisms responsible for Pavlovian conditioning but cannot provide much insight about the more relevant (to humans) memory phenomena such as learning how to do long division.

What can the neuroscientist contribute to help us understand this infinitely complex process? Very little, as yet. We are only beginning to understand the shape of the problem. Recognition that cerebral processing is holographic is both a help and a hindrance. It sets us in the right direction, but at the same time it is daunting to realize how little we know. Much of the work on specific neural circuits appears irrelevant to an explanation of these larger processes.

Recent developments in computer technology give some hope for eventual insights into the neural mechanisms of consciousness. Both the design of the computers themselves and, more especially, the writing of complex programs have brought renewed interest and attention to the mathematical theory of information processing. Linguistics, too, is fundamental to any consideration of symbolic communication, and computers have been both a tool and a stimulus to fundamental research in linguistics. Both linguistics and, more generally, the basic theory of all information processing shed some light on the larger problem of how the brain itself processes information.

The influence of these related disciplines has already provided some help. Computer engineers deal very directly with many of the same problems of coding and of information processing that we have mentioned. They have explored a concept that promises to help us understand our brains, the distinction between serial (step by step) and parallel (multiple simultaneous pathways) processing of information. Closely related to this distinction is another between what might be called "deterministic" and "statistical" functions. At the risk of making the confusion complete, I must point out that holographic processing, already discussed, is both "statistical" and "parallel." Thus there is a close, but as yet poorly understood, relationship between these three properties.

"Deterministic" functions of neuron networks are simply operations wherein the circuit is simple and the laws governing the operations are known and operate consistently, so that the whole system works in a completely predictable manner. Neurons often can be analyzed in terms of simple synaptic processes that, in effect, turn the neuron on or off like a switch. This kind of function, which is common in many biological mechanisms, is attractive to biologists, because it lends itself to easy modeling and computer simulation. For a mechanistic scientist it is comforting to be able to reduce living functions to such simple all-or-nothing events.

Not all neural mechanisms operate that simply, however. John von Neumann pointed out the paradox inherent in thinking of brains as deterministic machines. He asked how one could obtain such reliable, predictable behavior from cells that we know are exquisitely sensitive to subtle changes in metabolic, ionic, and other conditions. He asked a second, and related, question concerning the large-scale operations of large populations of neurons working in concert: How is it one can drink a cup of strong coffee, or an alcoholic drink, and thereby raise or lower the threshold of millions of neurons, but still be able to add two and two to get four, and, in short, to maintain a very predictable performance from the neural circuit?

Von Neumann's questions point out the difficulty of viewing neuronal networks deterministically, as if they were computer circuits, made up of stable, reliable components connected in unambiguous pathways. Neurologists have not always thought it necessary to cope with the alternative "statistical" approach to neuron function, and one reason they haven't is the fact that many neurons do indeed operate in a very stable and predictable fashion. Cellular neurophysiologists naturally choose to do their experiments on such systems, so scientific journals are filled with reports of simple reproducible experiments on the neurons of the lobster heart, or the mantle of a marine mollusk. Readers of such reports are left with the impression that all neuronal circuits are reliable, deterministic mechanisms, and in cases where the behavior of the system is erratic and variable, it is

thought to be the fault of the experimenter for not controlling the environmental conditions closely enough.

Even in higher organisms with large and complex
nervous systems, many simple reflex arcs do frequently operate in this satisfactory and predictable fashion. At the reflex level of nervous function, neural circuits can be very effectively mimicked by computer programs. Indeed, a reflex
arc strongly resembles a transistor logic circuit. Perhaps the
success of the "model builders" engaged in computer simulation of these more elementary regulatory functions is what
has enticed many theoretical biologists down the primrose
path of simplistic attempts to reproduce higher functions of
the brain with computer circuitry.

The major fallacy in such efforts is the neglect of a
fundamental difference between the simple reflex circuits of
the nervous system and the higher mental processes. The
sheer size and complexity of these latter systems, plus the
unreliability of the individual components alluded to by von
Neumann, make it impossible for them to operate by simple,
step-by-step, all-or-nothing, deterministic processes. Despite the impossibility of describing the exact nature of the
mechanisms used by the brain in these higher functions, a
few distinctions can be made between the two levels of neural function.

1. *Serial vs. parallel processing.* A simple reflex arc is a
pathway from the sensory receptor through one or more intermediate neurons, operating in predictable and reliable
ways to provide a stimulus to a muscle cell that completes
the reflex action. If you touch your finger to a hot stove, the
pain receptors in the skin will send a volley of nerve impulses up the arm to the spinal cord. The incoming sensory
nerves will synapse with intermediate neurons, which carry
the message to motor neurons a few millimeters away. The
motor neurons will then send a volley of excitatory impulses
to the flexor muscles of the arm, and the hand will be drawn
away from the stove. All of this happens in much less time

than the description takes. If the stove is very hot, the reaction may be quite violent, involving hundreds of neurons. Nevertheless, the circuit is simple and straightforward. All of the neurons behave the same way, and the information follows a linear sequence from sensory nerves to intermediate neurons to motor nerves. In this "serial processing" each step in the sequence follows the immediately preceding step. The redundancy of a large number of similar circuits provides an element of statistical reliability as well as a means of regulating the magnitude of the reflex action, but it does not increase the speed or the complexity of the fundamental process.

Parallel processing, on the other hand, requires separating the input information into a number of components, each of which is operated on simultaneously by different parts of the whole neural circuit. It is qualitatively different from mere redundancy in that the many parallel circuits are doing different things with the information. In the example of the hot stove, the major reflex mechanism was accomplished by a serial sequence of events. While the serial processing of the pain reflex was going on, some of the information would also ascend through branches of the intermediate neurons of the reflex circuit and reach the brain. Here the message would branch again and again, to occupy many different simultaneous, parallel pathways. Some would store the information about the painful experience in memory, so you would learn to avoid touching hot stoves in the future. Others might activate your conscious mind, and a few choice words might be emitted, testifying to the involvement of your language centers. Tears might be shed, if the pain was severe, and the heartbeat would speed up. All of these pathways are doing different things, and each is acting simultaneously with the others (though their durations might vary). This is not a very good example of parallel processing, for the results are not intimately coordinated, nor do they converge into one specific outcome. The more interesting cases of parallel processing are those like the transmission of form and pattern information from the retina to the brain, in which the input is divided, separate circuits process the information in ways that are continuously responsive to one another's activities, and all of the parallel paths eventually reunite to create some common outcome that could not have been achieved by any single serial sequence of processing.

We are not very familiar with complex parallel processing, in part because our computer technology has largely worked by means of serial pathways. Even though the information proceeds through the computer circuitry by means of a "bus" that may consist of eight, sixteen, thirty-two, or even more parallel pathways, the simultaneous transmission of a group of "bits" of binary information on the bus is not true parallel processing, for the set of bits makes up a single "byte" or word of command or of information, and the computer deals with each byte in a step-by-step serial order. It is true that larger computers are able to separate functions into different segments of the operating system and often carry on more than one function at a time, but this very elementary form of parallel processing does not represent a fundamental change of strategy. Any such example could be duplicated by holding the outcome of one stage of the program in storage while carrying on the other stages, and then finally recombining the results of the several steps, in a serial fashion. True parallel processing would involve a continual interaction among the various simultaneous pathways, with mutual influence on the intermediate stages of each element of the set. Figure 22 illustrates something of the complexity of visual information transfer by parallel processing. The face could not be "seen" by any conceivable program of point-by-point serial analysis.

2. *Deterministic vs. statistical behavior.* In a deterministic circuit the behavior of each neuron (or each transistor) can be accurately predicted from the knowledge of the input and the set of conditions obtaining. In the brain the variability of the neurons themselves, plus the sheer size and complexity of the interconnecting network, militates against any possibility that the higher functions work by a deterministic mechanism. Even computers above a certain size provide

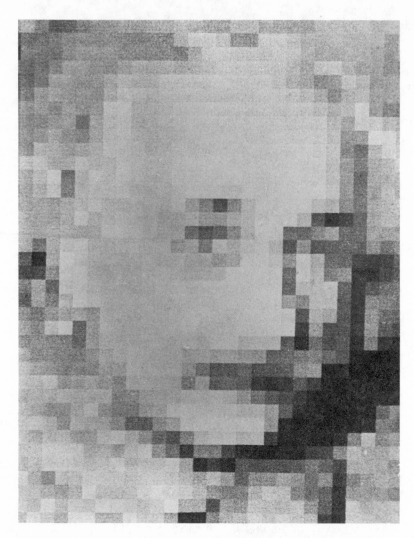

Figure 22. Demonstration of parallel processing in the visual system. This is a "digitized" image made up of uniform squares of varying darkness. Look closely at the picture. No amount of point-to-point serial analysis can reveal the pattern. Now hold the page at arm's length or, better, prop the book up and stand a dozen feet away. Immediately you will see a marvelously detailed portrait of a well-known scientist. Parallel processing by your visual system has generated a meaningful scene that does not really exist in the crude pattern of gray squares. Look again at the squares that depict the eyes in the portrait. There is nothing in the actual pattern to account for the fine detail that your mind was able to generate holistically. Although a computer was used to generate this image, no computer could be programmed to "see" the recognizable human face by any scanning of the individual squares.

many examples of nondeterministic functions. There is a group of elements in a computer called a register. Each part of a register stores a bit of information in the form of an electric charge. One could observe the charge state on any one of these devices as the program ran, and in fact, we sometimes do, by connecting a small light to each element of the register. The familiar panel of blinking red lights on a computer is one way we monitor the state of the registers during the program. The blinking of the lights reflects the very rapid series of charge changes as bits of information are put in and taken out of the register. Since the particular charge state of that one element of the register is essentially meaningless except in the context of the charges on the other elements of the register, and since the whole set of charges is conditional on the particular stage of the program, and finally, since the choice of which of several different registers to use depends on the particular state of the central processing unit, the activity of any one specific light, taken in isolation, is unpredictable, even though it is functioning in a meaningful way in the operation of the program. One would have to observe the activity of a whole ensemble of elements over a period of time to gain any meaningful information about the functions they were involved in. So in that sense we would have to concede that the instantaneous state of any particular light in the group, taken in isolation, is unpredictable, but not meaningless. It is in this same general sense that the functions of particular neurons during mental activity can be described as "statistical" rather than deterministic.

Both deterministic and statistical operations are carried out by neurons of the cerebral cortex. One line of neurophysiological research relies on the information obtained from electrodes implanted in the brain to observe the activity of single neurons. An experimental animal is anaesthetized, and a part of the brain is surgically exposed. Tiny electrodes are carefully lowered into a selected region of the brain until the electrical activity registered by the amplified output of the electrode itself indicates that the target neuron has been reached. In many cases the neuron responds in a regular and predictable fashion to a stimulus applied at some remote point by producing a pulse of electricity in the electrode. If the visual cortex is being explored, for example, the stimulus might be a small spot of light focused on the retina of the unconscious subject. In the simplest case, the neuron might fire every time the light was turned on. Or off. This is evidence for the existence of deterministic neural circuits in the brain. However, even when no specific stimulus is being supplied, these same neurons are often observed to fire in a random pattern, unrelated to any known state of activity.

One explanation of the "random" behavior is that neurons are multipurpose elements in the circuitry that makes up the brain, and any given element may be simultaneously involved in widely different functions, some of them simple and deterministic, others "statistical." It would be the "statistical" functions of huge populations of neurons that were responsible for the apparently random activity of individual cells, and with the limitations of our present technology there is no way we could analyze the "program" being processed by these large populations simply by observing the activities of individual members of the group, any more than we could analyze the program of a large computer by watching one light on the panel.

Other areas of neuroscience research examine directly the statistical kind of neural function, rather than observing the activities of single neurons. One such area is the study of *evoked responses* in the electroencephalogram. When the brain waves picked up by means of external electrodes on the scalp are analyzed by a computer, it is possible to retrieve a particular waveform from the apparently random electrical activity. The brainwave is associated with certain mental states, such as the recognition by the subject of a significant stimulus amid a series of meaningless stimuli. E. Roy John was among the first scientists to explore this kind of activity. He found that cats trained to respond to a certain stimulus generated a characteristic brainwave that he called the "readout component" every time they had to make a decision as to the proper response to the stimuli.[12] These waveforms are remarkably reproducible and can be found almost anywhere the electrodes are placed. Therefore we say that they are "global," which is a punning usage drawing on the usual meaning of "global" as "worldwide" but also referring to the spherical shape of the cerebral hemispheres. Global electrical activity of the brain is activity that is found all over the surface of the cerebrum and is not localized in any particular specialized region. It is important to realize that there are both regional and global kinds of electrical waves occurring simultaneously when the brain is active. This reflects the fact that neurons are multifunctional and are often simultaneously operating as a part of a small group of committed specialized elements and also as a part of a much larger population engaged in a completely different activity.

Perhaps the most interesting experimental evidence of global activities comes from a study of those electrical waves obtained by computer averaging of the electroencephalographic potentials taken from scalp electrodes on normal human subjects. One class of these waves, called "cognitive evoked potentials," is seen only when the subject is presented with a stimulus in which he or she recognizes some specific cognitive feature. For example, a group of short sentences is flashed on a screen, one by one, with some containing an unexpected or incorrect construction. There is often a specific electrical response to these "semantic incongruities." In another example, from our own laboratory, a subject is shown randomly flashing red or green lights. When the subject is told that she will win money every time the red shows, and lose on the green, a particular waveform appears after each stimulus. The waveforms are recognizable, one for "win" and another for "lose." Their shapes do not depend on whether winning is on the red or the green and thus are determined by the "meaning" of the stimulus and not its particular color. These experiments demonstrate direct electrophysiological evidence that extensive populations of neurons spread all over the cortex participate in the cognitive interpretation of sensory stimuli.

The brain is enclosed by tough membranes, layers of blood vessels, and the thick bones of the cranium. The electrical activity of single neurons is too small to be measured through all these layers. In order to be detected from external electrodes placed on the scalp, brain potentials must be made up of the combined and simultaneous activity of thousands of neurons. It is surprising that electroencephalography is possible at all. The evidence for simultaneous electrical activity in vast ensembles of cortical neurons suggests that a common mode of activity exists that is quite different from the sequential transfer of nerve impulses from one neuron to another, as in a reflex pathway. It is possible that these electrical signals reflect a pattern of information processing that is parallel, rather than serial. Until we know more about the actual neural states responsible for these "global" potentials, it is probably fruitless to speculate, in spite of the temptation to bring the "statistical" and the "parallel" properties of the brain into one unified hypothesis.

Despite the difficulties in describing parallel processing, one practical example in the brain is beginning to be understood. When visual information from the retina is transmitted to the occipital cerebral cortex, a number of parallel pathways carry different "features" of the complex pattern of stimulation. When you look at a straight line, for example, the information about the visual pattern projected onto the retina is encoded into messages about the straightness, the width, the brightness, whether it is vertical or horizontal, and so on. The way in which the visual pattern is broken down into separate components for parallel processing is extremely complex, and not enough is known about it to provide a completely satisfactory description, but the basic facts are as follows: The retinal cells appear to operate in fairly large groups, called a receptive field. Each rod or cone cell of the retina is a member of many different receptive fields, and each receptive field is made up of many rod and cone cells. The cells in the various receptive fields appear to combine their outputs in some special way to perform what is called a Fourier analysis on the visual pattern.

To make clearer how the eye processes visual information, let us compare it with the mechanism used in a television camera. The camera operates by scanning across one very narrow line of the scene focused on its "retina." The light-sensitive element acts like a photocell to generate a voltage that is proportional to the instantaneous brightness of each segment of the line it is scanning. Thus a plain black surface would result in a voltage of zero, while a uniformly bright surface would give a steady high voltage, and any scene that included both bright and dark areas would produce an irregularly varying voltage proportional to the changes of brightness encountered during the scan. This jagged wave of rapidly varying voltage can be modulated on a "carrier wave" and transmitted to the television receiver, where it is used to vary the brightness of the electron beam sweeping across the face of the television tube, and thereby it recreates the bright and dark areas "seen" by the scanner in the camera back in the TV studio. Of course one line would not make a very satisfactory picture, but the camera makes another scanning sweep immediately below the first, and then another and another until it has covered the whole area of the picture. All of this is accomplished in a small fraction of a second, so to our eyes the picture appears as if it had been produced as a continuous two-dimensional scene, instead of as a large stack of thin lines of varying brightness.

If you have followed this description you may recognize that video transmission is a case of serial processing. In effect, your television screen can be thought of as a very large number of tiny areas, starting in the upper left corner, and numbered consecutively like letters on a printed page to the bottom right corner. Each little area is activated in turn to a certain degree of brightness, and because of the speed of this serial process, it appears to our eyes as though the whole screen were illuminated simultaneously. The information is handled serially because there is only a single channel, and only one spot on the screen is activated at a time.

Imagine a different kind of television system in which the camera made a line scan and then performed a Fourier analysis on the waveform produced by the different levels of brightness. (A Fourier analysis reduces any varying wave to a discrete series of specific mathematical terms. Usually the series is infinitely long, but in practice it is possible to ignore all terms beyond the first few without loss of significant information. Fourier *synthesis* is the process of recreating the original waveform from the components of the series.) Then suppose each term of the Fourier series were transmitted simultaneously on a separate (parallel) channel to the TV receiver, where a Fourier synthesizer recreated the original waveform of the scan. The recreated waveform could produce instantaneously a line of varying brightness across the screen. We might as well assume that all the other lines of the picture were also simultaneously transmitted on their own sets of channels, so the whole picture could be produced instantaneously, instead of by a sequential series of sweeps. This system would represent parallel processing. It may not be obvious that such a technique would be any improvement over the serial transmission currently used. In fact, however, the efficiency of information transfer would be vastly greater. One would need many channels rather than just one, but each channel would carry only a single encoded number, representing the value of one of the terms of the Fourier series, and therefore the "bandwidth" of the channel could be very narrow, so there would be a net saving of room on the crowded radio spectrum. Even more important, the time it takes to transmit the message, consisting of a single number on each channel, would be very short—in fact, many thousands of times shorter than the time required to send one scan of a line on present television systems. Hence the speed of transmission of the whole picture would be very much faster. So fast, in fact, that one could send more than a hundred different pictures during the time interval now taken by the beam to make one complete sweep of the screen of your television tube. Thus each complete picture could be received and stored for the local electronic circuit to use in its leisurely scanning process to create one frame of a continuing series making up a specific program. The receiver could sort out the different programs, all of which are being received on one channel, and display whichever one was selected. (This system sounds so good, one wonders why we don't have it for our commercial television broadcasts. Alas, it is much easier to describe in principle than to actually design in working hardware. We have almost no knowledge of a technology for parallel processing.)

One characteristic of a parallel processing system is that each channel of the parallel processor is "decoded" in relationship to all of the other channels. The frequency and amplitude of one term of a Fourier series, received in isolation, would provide no meaningful information about a television picture. In contrast, one small segment of a single channel in the usual serial transmission of a television picture would provide all the information needed to produce one small segment of the total picture, and none of the rest of the transmission would add anything to the clarity or pattern of that portion already received. On the other hand, loss of all but the first few channels of a Fourier transmission would not cause the loss of any particular portion of the picture: The whole picture would be there, but the details would be fuzzy. The missing channels would be needed to provide the fine structure of the scene. (That is why we can discard all of the higher terms of a Fourier series without losing much information. Since each successive term gives finer and finer details of the whole picture, there is no use including any terms that make the picture better than the resolution of the final reproducer.)

Such a system is holographic, and the analogies to the photographic hologram, though not exact, are impressive. Human vision actually does work in some such manner. It is likely that no more than twenty parallel channels of Fourier terms are used to give us the marvelous resolution and detail that our eyes are capable of. The situation is complicated by the fact that we have a central region in our retina, the fovea, which has much finer and sharper vision than the peripheral parts of the retina can give. To see something very clearly, we move our eyes so that the object is projected on the foveal part of our retina. Thus we do not need such enormous resolving power over our whole visual field. Even so, it is incredible that such vast amounts of visual information can be transmitted with as few as twenty Fourier channels.

A look at the mathematics of information processing gives some explanation of how so few channels can transfer so much information. Consider the amount of information carried by ten different "channels" operating independently. Suppose each channel were an old-fashioned telegraph wire, and that the maximum rate of transmission of Morse code were just enough to specify a one-digit decimal number each second. Each channel would be unrelated to the others, so two channels would carry twice as much information as one, and ten would carry ten times as much. Therefore ten channels operating independently of one another would provide sufficient information to transmit ten unrelated numbers per second. Just to make this illustration more interesting, let us suppose you are receiving, in advance, the winning numbers in a betting game in which the odds are strictly equal. Knowing the correct number out of ten choices gives you odds of 10 to 1 and enables you to win $10 for every $1 bet. With ten channels you can win $100 for each transmitted signal.

On the other hand, consider the case of ten parallel channels operating together. Channel one would still provide one decimal digit. Channel two would provide the second digit of a two-digit number. The two numbers together would specify one number out of a hundred, so by the rules of the game you could win $100 with your $1 bet. Three channels would give you one number out of a thousand. Ten channels, transmitting cooperatively, would specify one number out of ten raised to the tenth power, which tells you the winning number out of 10,000,000,000, which with fair odds enables you to win $10,000,000,000 with your $1 bet! Thus parallel processing is unbelievably more efficient for information transfer.

Parallel processing of some sort undoubtedly occurs in the brains of many different species of animal. What I am suggesting is that the adaptation of some as yet poorly understood strategy of parallel processing is involved in the manipulation of symbols in the human brain, and that it is this adaptation that gives us our unique linguistic capacity, and with it, consciousness.

In the passage quoted in Chapter One, Sacher mentions a sudden increase in information processing capacity at a certain stage of evolution of the human brain. He suggests that "as of that moment the amount of cortex was no longer the limiting factor in man's cognitive apprehension of his environment, so that, also as of that moment, selection for increased brain size ceased."[3]

It does seem curious that the size of brains, which had been increasing drastically in the last 500,000 years of human evolution, has not continued to increase since the beginning of language. An adaptationist would argue that now, in a culture-dominated species, selection for increased braininess should operate more powerfully than ever. There is much evidence, some of which has been mentioned in the foregoing paragraphs, that we do not need all of the cortical neurons that we already have. Is it possible that a switch to parallel processing gave such an enormous advantage that we have not yet caught up to the information processing potential we already possess? It is a comforting speculation.

In this chapter I have tried to indicate, in a general way, the main ideas about the two most distinctive features of the human brain—its lateral specialization and the holographic/parallel/statistical nature of cerebral information processing. We are now, at last, ready to bring these ideas to bear on the issue this book addresses: how the linguistic faculty evolved. To do so requires one more step. It will be easier to talk about the neurological basis of language if we use the concepts of information processing. The next chapter will discuss how information from the sense organs is encoded and processed and then attempt to show how linguistic coding developed as a natural outcome of cross-modal processing of sensory information.

Information processing is a familiar concept in this age of computers. It is not difficult to accept that the brain functions as an information processor. Might the information-processing capacity be a long-sought-for definition of intelligence? We can measure information processing in various ways: by the speed, the volume (in terms of simultaneous channels), the accuracy, and the capacity to deal with many different forms of information. Are not these factors fair measures of what we call intelligence? It is fashionable to denigrate intelligence tests, but however poorly they may function as *definers* of intelligence, the actual qualities they measure are very close to the preceding list.

If we accept information-processing capacity as a definition of intelligence, or at least concede that they are intimately related, we are presented with a powerful tool for a better understanding of intelligence, for there exists a rigorous methodology for measuring all of these qualities of information processors. In the next chapter we will examine the formal rules for measuring information and see how the sensory brain, in particular, has yielded many of its secrets to this approach. From this start we can hope to generalize our understanding of how cognitive processes work.

Language and
Neural Codes

Therefore am I still
A lover of the meadows and the woods,
And mountains; and of all that we behold
From this green earth; of all the mighty world
Of eye and ear,—both what they half create,
And what perceive; well pleased to recognise
In nature and the language of the sense
The anchor of my purest thoughts, . . .

WORDSWORTH[13]

A DICTIONARY DEFINITION OF *information* gives "knowledge" and "instructions" as synonyms. Whenever knowledge or instruction is transmitted or processed, it must be put into some form that can be communicated. Information may be communicated in many ways—by a smell, a gesture, a series of electric pulses, a geometric pattern, a sound. All of these are codes.

Coding, in the ordinary meaning of the word, consists of translating information from one "language" into another. A foreign language is a code, as are computer languages, Morse code, ASCI (the modern teletype code), and hieroglyphics. In a more general sense, we should not think of coding as restricted to verbal information. Any kind of information can be encoded, not just words. Thus musical notation is a code for certain aspects of sound, and a few notes on a staff can be decoded by the mind of a musician to evoke the first bars of Beethoven's Fifth Symphony. A map is a code for certain spatial relationships, and a few lines on a piece of paper can create an image of a mighty cliff ringing a gentle valley. Most codes are not used for purposes of concealment or secrecy, but simply because information processing or transmission requires that the information be represented by a set of symbols.

Photography may be thought of as an encoding procedure, one in which a particular pattern of light and darkness is transformed into an arrangement of silver grains embedded in an emulsion. The pattern is decoded by simply looking at the gross distribution of the silver on a print and recognizing the light and dark areas as representations of the original brightness or darkness of a real scene. A photographic portrait of your grandfather is not a person, nor is it any exhaustive transcription of his qualities. It is a very small abstract of certain visual qualities at a certain instant of time. Lower animals show no signs of recognizing photographs of things they ought to be familiar with. Dogs are not interested in the pictures of dogfood on a can. We humans accept pictures so easily that we are often unconscious of what a feeble representation of reality a photograph really is. You might hand a snapshot to a friend and say, "That's my grandfather." The friend would never think of asking, "Your grandfather is a small piece of paper?" You both accept casually and unthinkingly the fact that a picture is an acceptable "code" for a person.

If we accept that codes exist for other kinds of information as well as for language, we can begin to examine the more universal aspects of coding. We are helped in this examination by the realization that information itself can actually be measured. This revolutionary idea was first thought of in 1948, when Claude Shannon of the Bell Telephone Laboratories published a paper in which he developed the mathematical theory of information.[14] Scarcely six months later Warren Weaver, recognizing the significance of the new ideas, published, with Shannon, a more general exposition of the theory.

The central ideas of information theory are so simple that they can be summarized in two statements:

1. Anything can be adequately represented by a series of binary digits.
2. The number of binary digits required for such representation is a measure of the quantity of information.

Each of these statements needs explaining. "Anything" means any kind of information, in any form. It means any message that is expressible in words, any picture, any sound, smell, electric potential—in short, *anything*. "Adequately" refers to the amount of detail or "resolution" you wish to transmit. No finite message can ever tell everything there is to know. Information must always be limited to what is deemed sufficient for the purpose. "This guy goes off to fight a war, and then has a lot of adventures on the way back home" is a schoolboy's message about a Greek hero. Homer's epic is a much more "adequate" message about the same man. For visual messages, the "grain" or resolution of a picture is what is meant by adequacy of representation. The decision about how much to include in the message is usually up to the "sender." Sometimes the receiver of the message may choose to ignore some of the information. In our sensory system the sender of information is the peripheral sense organ—for example, the ear. Sometimes the brain, as receiver of the information, simply "tunes out" or ignores a monotonous or uninteresting message, such as street noises outside your window.

The "atom" of information is the BIT, an acronym for BInary uniT. Binary digits are simply any number systems in which there are only two symbols—0 and 1, + and −, "on" and "off," dot and dash, nerve action potential and no action potential. The world is full of binary systems. Statement 1 simply says that it is possible to encode all sorts of information in the.form of a series of dots and dashes or electrical pulses or a pattern of all-or-nothing nerve impulses. That a binary code can be used to transmit information is not surprising in the case of verbal messages. We are already familiar with Morse code (although it could be argued that Morse code is not truly binary, since it requires three symbols if you include the space between groups). Pictorial information can be sent by television, and the electrical "message" from a television camera can be encoded in a series of binary pulses. Having information in the form of a binary "alphabet" makes it easy to measure, which brings us to Statement 2. Since the number of binary units (bits) in a given message is strictly proportional to the amount of information sent, counting bits gives a quantitative measure of the information.

After getting over the shock of thinking of information as a quantity that can be measured at all, we begin to wonder what use can be made of such a measurement. Biologists have learned that the concept of life as an information processing system leads to valuable insights. In the first chapter we talked about evolution as an accumulation of information—genetic or cultural. The accumulation of useful information is obviously a valuable asset. Being able to measure the quantity of information gives us a powerful tool for analyzing the information processing capabilities of both living and nonliving systems.

Even more important than simply accumulating information is the ability to process information rapidly and efficiently. According to Turing's Theorem, any computer can carry out any programmable process that any other computer is capable of handling. If this is true, why do many companies waste money spending many thousands of dollars for a big main-frame computer when a cheap "home computer" can do the same job? The answer is obvious. A calculation that the large computer does in less than a minute might take a thousand years for the more limited computer to finish, and constant attention by a human operator would be required to feed in the program and the raw data that the bigger computer could absorb in seconds and hold in its memory for the whole job.

The difference between a big expensive computer and a small cheap model is in the information processing capacity, and that ultimately comes down to speed and efficiency. But even in computers, speed and efficiency are not purely matters of "hardware." The program also determines how well a task is performed. In human terms, the "hardware" corresponds to the innate functional capacity of the brain, but the "software" is the program acquired through the learning and experience of the individual, and it is at least as important as the biological equipment. I suppose I could, after all, make as good a hand axe as my hypothetical Neanderthal friend, but it would take me many hours to do what he could accomplish in minutes. His brain and his muscles would be trained to handle the information about the size, grain structure, and cleavage planes of the flint efficiently, and his motor coordination, from long practice, would guide his blows with a minimum of effort and waste motion. I have a very much more powerful system of information processing than the Neanderthal had, but until I had acquired a proper "program" of skills my efforts would be wasteful of time, flint, and invective. It would be of little use to reflect on my superior knowledge of solid state physics, the chemical composition of flint, crystal structure, or the aesthetic principles of hand tools. What he would have that I lack is an efficient and specialized capacity to process the information necessary for the reduction of a flint nodule to a sharpened oval. My superior memory storage and retrieval abilities and my better strategy for generalized information processing are not enough to substitute effectively for his superior, though limited, programming.

Thus size and speed are not the only significant qualities to consider in judging an information processor. Proper programming is the other essential for maximizing its effectiveness. Computer design is perhaps somewhat ahead of programming technology, so most computer applications are much more limited by "software" inadequacies than by the "hardware." In the case of human evolution the same is probably true. Our mental "hardware" is capable of unimaginably better performance than we generally achieve, but our cultural programming is wasteful, inefficient, and obsolescent. The few cases in which we have learned to use our splendid brain at something approaching its maximum capability are quite impressive. Imagine the rate of information processing involved in, for instance, the playing of a rapid passage of music by an organist. Ten fingers and two feet are moving over the keys and pedals to produce hundreds of precisely timed notes per minute. By any standard of analysis, the feat is prodigious!

Since the capacity for processing information is the simplest measure we have for brain performance, a system for quantifying information provides a potential tool both for evaluating and understanding brain function. Unfortunately we have not yet been able to go very far with the measurement of information processing in the higher levels of mental activity. However, in the area of sensory physiology the concepts of information theory have been applied with great profit, both in the provision of better understanding of the sensory process itself and in giving insights as to how the brain functions as an information-processing device. Therefore we will examine the physiology of the senses in order to explore how the brain has achieved its capability for language.

To measure the information capacity of a sensory channel, we start with an analysis of what the sense organ is telling us. If, for example, we chose to examine a taste receptor specialized for sweetness, we might first determine how much the receptor is capable of telling us in the sensory message transmitted over its neurons. By tasting a variety of sweet things we could learn that although peppermint candy is different from chocolate, sweet is nothing but sweet. There are no variations in the subjective experience associated with the exposure of the receptor to a variety of substances other than differences in the *intensity* of the sensation. From this we might conclude that the message of the sweetness receptor was nothing more than a code for intensity. The description of the *quality* of sweetness is already taken care of by the "label" on the channel carrying the message.

Every sensory neuron has a specific destination in the brain. The area the neuron arrives at is activated by the incoming message to create a consciousness of the stimulus. The appreciation of what the stimulus is depends on the specialized location in the brain of these target neurons, rather than the nature of the "message" on the sensory neurons themselves. This fact was discovered long ago and was codified in the somewhat misnamed "Law of Specific Nerve Energies." The law states that whenever a sensory neuron is stimulated, regardless of how, the activity will be interpreted as a sensory stimulus of the appropriate modality. Thus if we apply an electric shock to the optic nerves by means of electrodes on the temples, the subject experiences flashes of light, rather than the sensation of a shock. If we squeeze a warmth receptor in the skin with tiny forceps, we feel a flash of heat, rather than a pinch. And when a brain surgeon stimulates a small area of the exposed sensory cortex, the patient "feels" a touch on the wrist, for instance, rather than a shock on his brain. What this tells us is that each sensory nerve fiber is a "labeled line" identified by the brain as being associated with a particular quality or "modality" of stimulus. Whenever a sensory neuron is activated, the brain assumes that the stimulus was an event appropriate to the specific sensory function of that particular neuron.

The use of a labeled line strategy results in a great savings in the length and complexity of the neural messages. Labeled lines are used in computers and in telephone systems for the same reasons. A leased wire from the racetrack to the betting parlor not only eliminates the need to dial the number, but it saves a great deal of conversation as well. "This is Joe. I'm calling from Arlington. In the first race, horse number three won, seven placed, and four showed." Compare that with a message on a "labeled line." "Race one: three, seven, and four." The difference is that the receiver of the message already knows by the label on the particular telephone that any message coming over that line will be from Joe at Arlington, and that it will be about the results of the race. Even greater economies could be made if desired. For instance, we could agree that each race would be reported in sequence, and so it would be unnecessary to mention the number of the race being reported: "Three, seven, four" would be the entire message.

When we apply this reasoning to the sweetness sensor of the taste buds, we see that the "message" does not need to contain any information about the quality of the stimulus other than its intensity. The "receiver" will already know who is at the other end of that line, and what he is reporting on, so a simple number signifying a certain level of intensity tells everything. (Vinegar could be 0, an apple, 5, and maple syrup, 10.)

Many of the simple sense organs of the body use nothing more than a labeled line and an intensity code for their messages to the brain. Thus it is possible to "crack the code" for these modalities of sensation. To actually measure the quantity of information needed for our sense of taste, for instance, we can do experiments on the range and resolution of our sweetness sensation. A number of subjects could taste different concentrations of sugar and agree on a minimum level of detection, a maximum concentration for saturation of the receptor, and how many steps of difference could be detected between these limits. Suppose there were, for most subjects, sixteen different concentrations of sugar that could be reliably discriminated by intensity, between the lowest concentration that could be tasted at all, and the highest concentration that produced any additional sweetness. The information content of such a system is exactly four bits. A single neuron with a potential maximum rate of firing of 1000 impulses per second could convey the whole message in exactly four thousandths of a second. An efficient code would be one in which the arrival or the non-arrival of an impulse in each millisecond represented a binary code symbol "1" or "0." Thus a set of four "0's" or "1's" provides a number from zero to fifteen for all the possible levels of taste intensity, by the following binary system:

Binary Code Group	Decimal Number
0000	0
0001	1
0010	2
0011	3
0100	4
0101	5
0110	6
.	.
.	.
1111	15

The total range of taste intensities, encoded in this fashion, can be reported with only four binary digits. Thus the information content of the system, or any system with only sixteen possible states, can be encoded in a four-bit message. Our friend Joe could report the winner of a race with a field of sixteen horses by simply tapping out "1001," which would mean "horse number 9."

Of course the nervous system doesn't use this particular binary code, nor is it optimally efficient in its information transfer. Biological receptors generally report intensity by the degree of activity of the neurons, and our sweetness neuron would carry bursts of nerve impulses of greater and greater frequency as the concentration of sugar increased. The upper limit to our sweetness sense might be set by the maximum capacity for carrying nerve impulses, perhaps around a thousand per second, and the lower limit or threshold of sensitivity is due to the random spontaneous activity of the neuron, or the "noise level." If the signal is less than the noise level, it cannot be detected. Below a certain concentration of sugar, the taste bud may still respond, but the message is ignored because it is indistinguishable from the activity of the neuron even when there is no stimulus at all. Actually, in the real case, it is likely that there will be many thousands of similar taste receptors and neurons, all sending the same message, and in such instances, the receiver can average all the inputs and determine that something is happening out there even though any individual neuron might be firing at approximately its noise level. From this we might predict that the number of receptors stimulated, as well as the intensity of the stimulus itself, should be significant in determining our lower threshold of detectability. Such is the case. A small drop of weak sugar solution is harder to taste than a whole mouthful of the same solution. A tiny dot of ink is harder to see than a large spot of the same intensity.

We have achieved a fair level of understanding of the coding mechanisms of those sense organs that utilize a labeled line system with a simple intensity code consisting of nerve impulses with higher and higher frequencies as the stimulus becomes stronger and stronger. However, when we get to the more complex senses, the code itself becomes much more complicated. In sound, for example, the intensity is what we call loudness. But sound has more than just loudness to be reported to the brain. There is also pitch. What kind of neural code is required to transmit information about two different features of the stimulus, loudness and pitch?

We shall look at some of the coding problems associated with the senses of hearing, vision, and olfaction in order to approach the question of how the brain evolved the complex symbolic codes that ultimately led to the linguistic capacity. Each of these three senses required a separate kind of neural code, as each was devoted to the reporting of entirely different kinds of information.

In the nineteenth century Helmholtz, Ohm, and others analyzed the auditory system. They attempted to reduce the neural code for sound to a simple intensity code by assuming that the sound vibrations were detected by different parts of the cochlea for each different frequency. Thereby the problem of pitch detection was taken care of by a labeled line mechanism. Each individual hair cell receptor (of which there are thousands) along the cochlea was thought to transmit its message to the brain over a specific neuron which carried a label saying, "I report on middle C." "I report A#." I'm Gb ." Since the pitch would be indicated by the specific location on the cochlea that originated the message, the coding system was required only to report the intensity of that particular component of the total stimulus. The only thing that remained for the researchers to argue over was the mechanism by which the sound waves were broken down in the cochlea to their various pure frequency components.

Unfortunately, it doesn't work that way. Sensory physiologists are still arguing about the mechanism, but the "place theory" of coding for pitch is inadequate. It is true that sensitivities for different pitches are distributed along the cochlea. However, when local regions of the cochlear receptors are destroyed, as they are in many cases of "nerve deafness," a literal interpretation of the place theory requires that the hearing for those specific frequencies belonging to the injured region should be completely absent. In fact, cochlear injuries do not produce any detectable loss in pitch perception, nor do the victims of such damage find any "missing" frequencies in their auditory experience. What is changed is the ability to hear the affected frequencies at low intensities. "Tone deafness" is always relative, not absolute. If the sound is loud enough to overcome the loss in sensitivity, the pitch information seems to be encoded as well as ever. Thus the pitch perception does not depend on the existence of a specific labeled line for each detectable frequency, and the code must somehow provide for both the amplitude and the pitch information in the overall pattern of the nerve impulses.

It is beyond the scope of this discussion to present the actual code systems that have been proposed to account for both loudness and pitch information in the auditory system. The matter is still being argued by research workers, and no detailed model meets universal acceptance. For our purposes it is sufficient to point out that all models for auditory coding that are taken seriously have the characteristics of a multi-path system in which the information is broken down into several independent components, transmitted on separate, parallel channels, and then ultimately reassembled in the brain to provide the conscious perception of the original sound. Thus it is a "holographic," "parallel processing," "statistical" code.

Vision is an even more complex problem, and the visual code has been studied with even more vigor than the auditory code. The visual receptors have to report on form, brightness, pattern, and color. Early theories relied on a simplistic model in which the mosaic of receptors in the retina simply reported their stimulation in an elementary intensity code, and the position and particular color sensitivity of the receptors provided color and pattern information by a two-

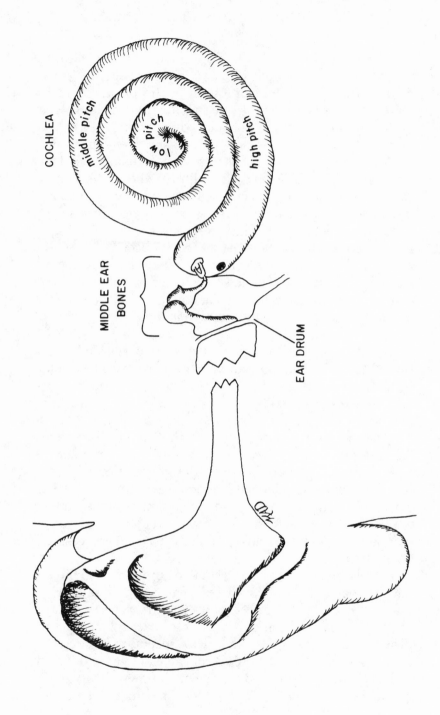

COCHLEA

middle pitch

low pitch

high pitch

MIDDLE EAR
BONES

EAR DRUM

dimensional "place" theory that is a variant of the labeled line strategy used in the more primitive sense organs. We now know that the situation is much more complex than that: The retina is actually a part of the brain and does a great deal of processing of the visual information before sending it down the optic nerve to the rest of the brain.

Again, the details are too complex for inclusion here, but the current models for visual coding employ the concepts of multiple-channel parallel processing. A pattern of light, darkness, and color—say the ruins of Tintern Abbey, being viewed by Wordsworth before he wrote the lines that begin this chapter—is projected onto the retina by the lens of the eye. The information about form and color is analyzed, broken down into a number of discrete features for transmission over parallel channels, and ultimately reassembled in the brain for the creation of an intelligible pattern of visual experience. Thus it is truer than Wordsworth could have realized that the "mighty world of eye and ear" is half perceived and half created. The "language of the sense" is not a passive report, but an active analysis and resynthesis of what is perceived.

Although it is true that a kind of mapping of the visual field occurs on the surface of the visual cortex of the occipital lobe of the cerebrum, that mapping is not a simple point-to-point correspondence between a particular retinal cell and a particular cerebral neuron. If there were no complex visual code, and the retinal cells just had direct lines to their corresponding cortical target cells, the scene projected onto the retina would simply be transferred to the surface of

Figure 23 (opposite). A diagram of the cochlea. The actual conversion of sound waves into a pattern of nerve impulses takes place in the cochlea. About 50,000 "hair cells" are arranged in several parallel rows along the length of this snail-shaped organ. The fact that different regions of the cochlea are "tuned" to different frequencies of sound led many investigators to believe that the perception of pitch was encoded according to the position of the specific hair cell along the length of the cochlea. These "place theories" of hearing are now considered inadequate.

the brain. But then there would still remain the problem of who "sees" the pattern on the cortex after it gets there. What is "that inward eye" of the poet? Fortunately, although the coding is much more complex, it does provide a way out of the quandary of infinite regression posed by a "television screen" model for visual transmission to the cortex.

The sense of smell, although it is the least well understood of the complex senses, also requires more than a simple intensity and place code for its information processing. Early workers assumed that olfactory receptors worked very much like taste receptors, with which they are related in their evolutionary and embryonic development. Taste experience relies on four separate kinds of receptors—sweet, sour, salty, and bitter. Our whole range of perception consists of nothing more than a blending of these four primary sensations in various degrees of intensity. With a little practice we can distinguish the two elementary components in a "sweet-sour" mixture and identify them as ordinary sweetness and ordinary sourness added together. By contrast, color vision employs a much more integrated strategy for the creation of new color experience from the blending of separate components. A mixture of yellow and blue creates a whole new sensation, called "green," in which a naïve observer would never guess the experience of "yellow" and of "blue" lay embedded. This difference provides a practical test for distinguishing between simple addition of independent sensations and true parallel transmission of sensory information.

At a more profound level, the difference provides some insights into the nature of parallel, "holistic" information processing itself. To return to the example of the photographic hologram, one small change in the scene—say a fly landing on an object being photographed—causes the "message" to be altered in every part of the hologram, not just the local region where the fly landed. Similarly, a change in the amount of yellow causes the whole experience of greenness to be altered, whereas in the taste sense, which is not holographic, decreasing the amount of sugar in a sweet-sour recipe leaves the sourness component unaffected. To return to the case of olfaction, many experimenters have assumed, without any real evidence, that smell also works by means of "primaries," which add together in the same way that the primary colors add to create new tints. Much of the scientific study of the sense of smell has been devoted to a search for the primaries. So far, none of the results have given any satisfactory insights into the coding of olfactory stimuli. Smell has turned out to be the most difficult of the senses to understand. Nobody has the slightest clue as to how the information is encoded. If there are a set of primary receptors that, like color receptors, blend their output in various proportions, the olfactory primaries must be much more numerous than the visual. At least fifteen or twenty are needed, according to some calculations. There are so many flaws in a "primary" theory of olfactory coding that we would gladly give it up entirely and look for a totally different mechanism but for the fact that the only two alternative possibilities are even more unlikely.

At the one extreme, we could assume an independent receptor population for each and every specific odor. Since we can reliably identify at least 50,000 different smells, a separate receptor for each would use up almost all of the receptors we have. The whole olfactory epithelium measures only about six square millimeters in area. Moreover, since new organic molecules are being synthesized almost daily, many of which have a unique smell, it seems unbelievably foresighted of nature to provide us with specific receptors for an odoriferous substance that never existed in our evolutionary history.

The other alternative for a coding mechanism is to have only one population of receptors, all alike. Each receptor would then "examine" the molecule of smelly substance and encode a complex message telling the brain what the olfactory experience should be. The major problem with such a theory, apart from the difficulty in imagining such an involved receptor mechanism, is that in order to describe 50,000 different smells, the code itself would have to be so complex that the transmission time would be much longer than it actually takes for olfactory perception.

Since no one has thought up any further alternatives for a coding mechanism, elimination of these two brings us back to a system that consists of a modest set, perhaps fifteen or twenty, of primary receptors, each of which reports on a certain specific "feature" of the molecules that come in contact with the olfactory membrane. These features would be transmitted to the brain, where they would be blended, like colors, to create a new experience in which the original components are not individually perceived.

This theory has difficulties too, although it is almost universally accepted. For instance, the behavior of the olfactory mechanism at very low concentrations of the odorant presents a problem. It can be shown that at near-threshold levels of certain substances, the actual number of molecules reaching the receptors on the surface membrane of the olfactory epithelium is so small that statistically it becomes quite unlikely that every different receptor type would be hit. If one or more receptors were missed there would be a false message to the brain, and the smell experienced would be quite different. If we let letters of the alphabet stand for the primary odors, imagine a smell that should create a message *apple*. If the "p" receptor were missed at low concentrations, the message received would be *ale*. In actual fact this never happens. Olfactory perception is amazingly accurate, and if you can smell the substance at all, you smell it correctly. We never find that at very weak concentrations an apple suddenly appears to smell like beer. The few cases where odors do change with concentration do so at the very high end of the concentration scale, never at the low end.

So in fact we really know almost nothing about the olfactory code beyond the fact that it is complex, like hearing and vision, and that it provides a very rich and varied set of subjective sensations that can be triggered by incredibly small numbers of airborne molecules. But whatever we discover about olfaction, its code will be very different from the codes for hearing and vision. Hence we know that the vertebrate nervous system has been able to generate at least three different complex neural codes, in addition to the more primitive intensity code used for the transmission of information from the simple senses. Even in the case of those "simple" senses there are complications in the information processing, although the complexities are more at the central nervous system level than at the peripheral sense organ itself. Aristotle, who is responsible for the persistent myth that we have only five senses, lumped together a group of sense organs of which he had little knowledge except by introspection. He called them "touch." Touch is not a sense, in either the physiological or anatomical meaning of the word. A whole group of different senses located in the skin are sensitive to heat, cold, pressure, stretch, pain, and perhaps other modalities of stimulation. The individual responses of these various organs can be integrated by the nervous system to provide an intuitively unified experience that we call touch. For example, the difference in our apprehension of the texture of a velvet cloth and of a marble stone is a complex combination of the signals from muscle stretch receptors, deep and superficial pressure receptors, and temperature receptors. There is no such thing as a "texture receptor."

For some of the senses, a part of the sensory message is information as to where on the body the stimulation is occurring. It is difficult to imagine experiencing a touch without knowing what part of your skin is being touched. (By contrast, smell, hearing, and some other sensations appear to happen "out there," rather than being consciously localized to a specific tiny region of our own bodies.) The term given to this property, when such distinctions were first being studied, was "epicritic." Epicritic senses carry the information about localization as a part of the message. The coding mechanism for localization of a stimulus is more complicated than one would guess. It is not merely a matter of "knowing" which nerve fiber the stimulus is carried by, although that is obviously an important part of the information processing. In humans, at least, the position data are perceived not merely in terms of our own body surface, but also in external space. Thus a bee sting on the calf of the right leg is localized both to a specific patch of skin and also to a particular location where that leg happens to be: "Alice's right foot, hearthrug, near the fender."

The evolution of human hands, with the greatly enhanced mobility and sensitivity of our fingers and the development of a fine coordination for tool making and tool use, has gone along with the evolution of a vastly improved position sense, both for our motor brain and our sensory brain. A consciousness of the position in external space, as well as the knowledge of what part of our own body is being stimulated, is a very important element of our sensory processing. The ability to tell the difference between, say, a pyramidal block and a cube by "touch" alone does not seem remarkable to us. If we could feel only the sharpness of the angles, without tracing with our fingers the directions of the flat planes, the task would be more difficult. A little reflection will convince you that what goes on in the mind as you make your tactile exploration of the blocks is a reconstruction in "visual" space of the external shapes and that you are very little concerned with the particular areas of skin that are actually being stimulated. (In fact, the very words *cube* and *pyramid* betray the visual bias of our sensory brain. If we were really thinking in tactile terms, we might call them "eight blunt corners, six smooth faces" and "four sharp corners, four smooth faces," respectively.)

The projection into the real space of the external world of localized sensory stimuli from the various skin and muscle receptors is called the "haptic sense." It is not a sense, of course, but a mental construct. This ability, although it evolved much earlier than the other special human adaptations, is crucially important to the development of a linguistic brain. Haptic processing is very intimately related to our visual sense, and, in fact, there is a good deal of overlap in the anatomical regions of the cerebral cortex that serve the visual and the haptic functions. Probably the haptic ability evolved as the earliest example of true interaction of sensory information from several different kinds of sense organs.

Interactions of this sort are known as cross-modal processing. "Mode" refers to a particular sensory system, and, as each sense has its own specific and unique code, there must be some sort of translation mechanism, at least in the formal sense, before two different languages can be used in a common processing center. Cross-modal processing has been recognized by almost everyone as being somehow connected in a vital way to the development of language. Unfortunately, the attractiveness of adaptationist theories about the evolution of speech has deflected most of the authorities from pursuing this promising lead to its logical implications about the biological, rather than cultural, genesis of linguistics.

Of course we cannot know the common code that integrates information from muscle, joint, and skin receptors for our haptic experience. Probably it resembles that used by the visual processing centers, since the result of all this haptic processing is subjectively almost indistinguishable from *seeing* a cube or a prism. (Our language, too, is extraordinarily visual in its bias. Thus we might say, "I *visualize* this as a cube" even when we are feeling it in the dark.)

Now that we have examined the different kinds of sensory codes, we can look for general principles that might help us understand linguistic coding in the brain. When we think of sensory·information as a literal coded message, as it certainly is, the difficulty of processing information across the "language barrier" of different sensory systems becomes apparent. We do not appreciate the complexity of this ability because the human, alone of all animals, has a brain that is specifically and uniquely suited to make the translations. That is, in fact, exactly what we mean when we say that our brain has a linguistic capacity. It is the possession of a *common modality* of symbolic processing that makes both cross-modal and linguistic processing possible. We find cross-modal processing so easy and natural that it has taken generations of psychologists and literally thousands of failed experiments to convince us that lower animals lack that ability.

Thus it is probably a combination of two tendencies that has delayed our recognition of the biological mechanisms responsible for the evolution of our language capability. The first is the insistence on an adaptationist paradigm, which placed speech ahead of the neurological changes as the major spur to language evolution. The second is the anthropomorphic habit that impedes our recognition of the importance and uniqueness of cross-modal processing. Even today few go as far as David Premack in acknowledging how intimately sensory processing and language are related. In an article on language capabilities of apes, he says:

> Differences between the human brain and the brains of other primates suggested that apes would be unable to form intermodal associations. It was proposed that, on this basis alone, speech would be possible only in man, since words *are* intermodal associations [emphasis added].[15]

Premack goes on to say that apes do show some capability for visual-haptic intermodal association, which would not be very surprising in the higher primates, but even here the evidence is far from conclusive.

We have finally arrived at a recognition of the critical importance of cross-modal information processing in the evolution of language. The increasing capability for using abstract symbols for information processing in the brain arose as an "accidental" consequence of an evolutionary trend for greater and greater integration of information from different sensory systems, and not from selection pressure for more spoken communication. If the unique cultural characteristics of Neanderthal influenced this development, then his tool-making and manipulative skills, rather than his need for communication, probably had the greatest relevance.

The evolutionary development that led to an increased competence for intermodal associations was, in fact, the "missing link" in the evolution of language and consciousness. Language evolved not as a result of selection for better and better communication between individuals but rather as a case of "exaptation" resulting from the evolution of better sensory interaction.

To visualize how the connection between intermodal processing and language developed, let us imagine a neural network designed to communicate among several discrete sensory inputs, each of which had its own specialized and unique code. The visual input line tells about form and color. The auditory channel refers to pitch and loudness, neither of which can have any conceivable meaning in the language of the visual processors. Then there is an olfactory input that reports in a language that neither the visual nor the auditory paths can possibly understand. What is the poor brain to do to bring these different, mutually incompatible classes of information together for some common processing step? There is no way that these disparate inputs can be fed into any common processor without being translated into a code that is capable of handling all of the modalities at once. What might that code be? It cannot talk about sights or sounds or smells. Such information would be meaningless to all but the specialized portion of the sensory brain that had always been committed to each of these senses. It cannot, in short, be a code that deals with sensory signals emitted by some outside agent. It must be a code that refers to the thing *itself*, not the stimuli it emits. The new code symbol would not be "small, black and white, furry," nor "pitter, patter, snuffle, stomp," nor yet "awful, acrid smell!" The code would have to be a symbol that stood simply for *skunk*—a symbol for the external reality itself, rather than a set of partial sensory reports *about* the outside world. Sensory codes consisted entirely of adjectives, and this universal cross-modal code introduced *nouns*. By the same cross-modal process the nervous system developed a code that integrates individual messages from muscles, stretch receptors, and again the eye, to move beyond the body with a symbolic code that refers to space and movement in the world outside of the skin, rather than angles of joints and stretch of muscles. Thus verbs were born.

The evolution of a neurological program capable of manipulating symbols that stand for real objects in the outside world and movements in real space outside of the body created an inherent capability for what we now call language, and this selfsame ability to manipulate the symbols in a logical and orderly way conferred upon our astonished Neanderthal a capacity for an inner stream of experience that we call consciousness. But this consciousness, unlike that of an awake cat, was no longer merely the perception of sensory stimuli. It emancipated all who followed from the dependence on chance arrival of real skunks to bombard the sensory receptors with stimuli. Given a set of symbols and the apparatus for manipulating them, consciousness permitted the invention of events internally. By a simple act of will we can conjure up the sight, sound, smell, or feeling of a skunk, where no real skunk exists. We can give him wings! We can dress him in blue denims, name him Jimmy, and have him play out a whole series of adventures with his friend Peter Rabbit.

After the biological evolution of the intermodal symbolic-processing capability that we can now call consciousness, selection pressures favored the rapid additional biological changes in tongue, palate, and throat structures we see in the transitional Neanderthal fossils. Logically these would be useless without a concurrent cultural evolution of specific spoken languages. This hypothesis nicely disposes of the chicken-and-egg paradox of which came first, language or consciousness. The adaptationist theory proposes that language capacity was selected for by the need for communication between individuals but fails to explain what they would have to communicate without the already existing internal symbolic processing we call consciousness. Human languages, like flying, could develop only after the necessary neurological structures were already evolved. The pressures that selected for these structures could not operate on hope but could be explained only in terms of an immediate utility.

Cross-modal processing is of itself a valuable asset, and one could use the adaptationist argument to justify its evolution in a tool-making, investigative biped. However, a stronger argument uses a deeper level of explanation based on the particular kinds of neurological changes that were already well started even before the first Neanderthals were on the scene.

Since no other animal has followed this particular evolutionary path, it is unlikely that cross-modal processing is possible without the other specific developments we have been describing in our discussion of the human brain. The kinds of cerebral organization described in the last chapter are not well enough understood as yet to suggest any more detailed speculation. Yet it seems that the strategy of information processing necessary for the generation and manipulation of a complex symbolic code of the sort we have been considering is almost inherent in the parallel-processing, holographic mode of operation that we know was already developing in our most immediate pre-human ancestors. Thus toward the end of the last interglacial period three separate but strongly interacting evolutionary developments were taking place in the brain of the late Neanderthals. The lateral specialization of the cerebral hemispheres, the increasingly holographic interactions of the cortical neurons, and the greater and greater integration of separate sensory modalities all converged to create an unexpected breakthrough. What emerged was—Adam.

Apes and
Little Green Men

As I listened from a beach-chair in the shade
To all the noises that my garden made,
It seemed to me only proper that words
Should be withheld from vegetables and birds.

A robin with no Christian name ran through
The Robin-Anthem which was all it knew,
And rustling flowers for some third party waited
To say which pairs, if any, should get mated.

No one of them was capable of lying,
There was not one which knew that it was dying
Or could have with a rhythm or a rhyme
Assumed responsibility for time.

Let them leave language to their lonely betters
Who count some days and long for certain letters;
We, too, make noises when we laugh or weep:
Words are for those with promises to keep.

W. H. AUDEN[16]

WE HUMANS TAKE PRIDE in our superior intelligence, delight in our free will, and glory in the richness of our language. We are not surprised that the writer of Genesis has God saying to Adam, "Have dominion over the fish of the sea, and over the fowl of the air, and over every living thing that moveth upon the earth." But Adam and his descendants have had to pay a price for such superiority: It is lonely at the top. To break out of this loneliness we have always claimed a kinship to other species of animals in myths and stories, peopled our world with sentient spirits, and shared our hearths, our food, and our affections with furry, feathered, and sometimes even scaly creatures outside of the family of man.

Anthropomorphism is an almost irresistible impulse. We all attribute human qualities to our pets. Perhaps because language and consciousness bubble up so naturally in the human child we regard such capabilities as inevitable and uncritically assume that there is a continuum in the level and quality of consciousness running from ourselves down to the humblest of organisms that have any brain at all. Our vocabulary reflects this assumption. We have never bothered to invent words that adequately distinguish between the human mental state and that of lower organisms. "You hurt that poor tree with the lawnmower." "My dog likes Sundays." "The cat knows when you're trying to study."

Science-fiction writers show a curious lack of imagination when they create extraterrestrial beings who not only have bodies made up of a hodgepodge of terrestrial appendages, but who also speak, think, and act in ways that are completely familiar to us as humans. Our human consciousness is all we know. The way *we* see things is the way things must be. So whether it be ants or tentacled monsters from Arcturus, we imagine them as basically people, give or take a few features.

However, when we recognize the special "accidental" quality of the evolutionary history of our human linguistic capacity, we begin to realize that many of our anthropomorphic assumptions cannot be supported. Perhaps we are truly alone and our isolation applies not only to our thoughts, but to our feelings as well. Although emotions are more primitive than consciousness and may be found in nonhumans, we cannot be sure that the experience of grief, pain, affection, and joy in lower animals is akin to the rich emotional life that is so much a part of our humanity. We recognize pain, sorrow, and eagerness in our pets and project all of our human feelings into them, without ever knowing what dog love or cat anger is really like.

Anthropomorphism is a major barrier to our understanding of the true nature of "consciousness" in nonhumans. Scientists, like all other humans, have this bias. We may be convinced that the brains of dogs, rats, and even chimpanzees are so different that those animals cannot possibly think like people, but by the same token we ourselves are totally incapable of thinking like a dog, rat, or chimpanzee, so we interpret their behavior in the only terms we know—human terms. As mentioned earlier, our language itself exacerbates the situation. Our whole vocabulary is naturally oriented to human experience, human needs, and human ways of sensing our environment. Richard Adams is one of the very few writers who have faced the problem at all effectively. In his splendid fantasy *Watership Down*,[17] he tries to transport his readers into the world of rabbits, rather than make his rabbit characters entirely like people. He invents a new vocabulary for matters that he fancies should be more important to rabbits than they are to humans, and by this clever device he convinces his readers that we are really entering the world and the consciousness of Fiver, Hazel, and the other "people" of his story. (For they really are humans, despite the artful concealment of the anthropomorphism of his novel.)

There are many ways in which human language predisposes us to anthropomorphic thinking. Our sight-dominated vocabulary, for example, severely limits our ability to appreciate the world of the smell-oriented dog. Nor can we really understand how a bat perceives the location, size, and motion of a flying insect from ultrasonic echoes. Never having fully known these kinds of sensory experience, we do not miss them. Difficult as it is to imagine sensations we do not experience, it is even harder for us to appreciate the world of an animal that lacks the richness of sensory perceptions that we enjoy. This is particularly true since we know that dogs and bats do, in fact, have eyes, ears, and noses, and so ought, in principle, to have the same sorts of sensory contact with the world as we do. We easily overlook the fact that our enormous visual cortex not only dominates our conscious mind but literally gives us an unimaginably greater variety and intensity of visual experience than other animals can achieve.

It is interesting to speculate on what sort of technology we might have developed, given, say, the bloodhound's olfactory apparatus. Instead of a tape measure, we might carry a small box of musk. To measure the length of a table, we would open the box at one end of the table, walk to the other end, and sniff. "Six feet, three inches," we would say, or whatever units might be appropriate for olfactoring distances. Painting a room would be done for the proper smell, rather than color. "I'm having the kitchen done in bacon, the living room in lilac, and the library in musty leather."

No, we cannot take seriously the proposition that any mind might work by other than visual imagery. Yet it is extremely unlikely that other species, even if they did develop a consciousness, would think in ways recognizable to us.

Among the contemporary primates, the chimpanzee and the gorilla are the two most closely related to humans. We naturally use these animals to study the question of whether our linguistic capability really is unique. Despite the wide evolutionary gap that separates us from these species, their general similarities to humans in form and movement create an even greater tendency to regard them as people. If it is difficult to resist a surge of affection for an eager puppy licking your hand, it is nearly impossible not to respond to a juvenile chimpanzee clinging like a baby in your arms. We read human expression into their serious, worried little faces, and no amount of scientific detachment can erase the powerful emotional bonds of kinship that inevitably develop between us. Recognition of this bias makes it difficult to criticize research workers in the field of primate intelligence for their tendency to attribute human qualities to their furry charges.

Nevertheless, it must be admitted that many of the early studies on the language capabilities of nonhuman primates did err in favor of the apes. And possibly because of the loneliness of our species, the lay public was eager to read and believe the reports that genuine verbal communication had been achieved with other animals. As we have learned more, both about language and about apes, our studies have become more critical, and there has been some retreat from the optimism of the earlier studies.

Since the hypothesis outlined in this book asserts that language is a uniquely human faculty, it is important to establish just how much linguistic capacity we can find in nonhuman subjects if we are to understand our own achievement. That apes can be taught to use "language" of some sort to communicate fairly effectively with their trainers is clear. To deny that these animals have a genuine linguistic capability requires that we show how their neurological mechanisms differ from ours when they communicate by means of symbols.

Two important distinctions are necessary for this discussion. The first is between communication and language. In a loose sense we can use the word *language* for any communication of information, but the more specific meaning of the word *language* cannot apply to the wide variety of smells, movements, colors, stridulations, bellows, or shrieks that function as genetically programmed signals in the animal world. The distinction is not always a simple one. Even we humans, with the gift of true language, rely heavily on nonlinguistic communication—facial expressions, "body language." The problem is that with the enormous power and flexibility of our language, we are able to verbalize every signal we give or receive, so we often confuse the linguistic *description* of the signal for the signal itself and thus fail to recognize the importance of nonverbal communication. Essentially the same message can be conveyed by the word *smile* as by the upturning of the corners of the mouth.

The second distinction is the one already mentioned, between vocabulary and syntax. Words all by themselves do communicate ideas, so it is easy to overlook the overwhelming importance of the rules of syntax that permit the generation of infinitely more complex messages than the isolated symbols could convey. "Banana!" signaled by an ape does communicate, but not as fully as, "Please go out of the room and get me a banana." "Ripeness is all" conveys an immensely richer message than that implied by the three words taken individually. Failure to observe the importance of these two distinctions was largely responsible for the mistaken optimism about the ability of apes to learn language.

Syntax, rather than words, is the most human accomplishment. Vocabulary is easy to acquire. A vocabulary is simply a set of symbols, and though symbols are obviously essential for language, by themselves they do not make a language. In a fundamental sense, all information processing uses symbols, for information is *about* things, and not the things themselves. Genes are the carriers of genetic information. The gene itself is not a trait but a coded message that can be "read" by the machinery of the cell to produce the traits that the genes govern. Yet we do not think of the genes as a language, except in a metaphorical sense. The open beak of a nestling is another kind of symbol that releases a certain instinctive pattern of feeding behavior on the part of the mother bird. There is communication by means of symbols, but communication is not the same thing as language.

Apes have a surprising ability to learn a vocabulary of arbitrary symbols that stand for actions, things, or qualities that they already "comprehend." Chimpanzees can apparently be taught to use these symbols in an appropriate way, whether they are "sending" or "receiving" the message. Syntax, however, is beyond the ape's comprehension. The symbols are manipulated in a lawless manner, with no apparent appreciation of the significance of sequence, juxtaposition, or interrelationship. When we read that chimpanzees compose messages like "Please go out of the room and get me a banana," it is easy to believe that they have demonstrated a genuine mastery of language. Such reports, although given in good faith, leave out several crucial points. One is simply the error inherent in data selection. A typical experimental session with a chimpanzee might take several hours, during which hundreds of symbols are used. A much more common message generated by the animal might be "Banana me banana get please banana out room," which is not a very convincing "sentence." It is hard to evaluate such utterances as examples of language. We simply do not have a satisfactory statistical measure for determining whether occasional "correct" sentences in an outpouring of symbols indicates a significant comprehension of a syntactical relationship between the signals the animal is broadcasting.

An even more important point that is sometimes overlooked in the evaluation of these language studies is a phenomenon known as the "Clever Hans effect." Der Kluge Hans was a horse who was trained in 1904 by a retired German schoolteacher, Wilhelm von Osten. Hans would tap the answers to questions with his hoof by a letter and number code. He could combine letters into words and sentences and could solve problems in arithmetic. The impressive performance attracted widespread attention among serious scientists. Herr von Osten was not an entertainer, but a sincere man interested in the process of education. He was also, obviously, a superb animal trainer. When Oscar Pfungst, from the Psychological Institute of the University of Berlin, studied the case, he discovered that the horse was responding to unconscious signals from his trainer, most notably an almost invisible "relaxation jerk" of von Osten's head when Hans had reached the correct number of taps.

Unlike recent charlatans like Yuri Geller, who dress up their modest ability as parlor magicians with claims of genuine magical powers,* von Osten was evidently unaware of his unconscious cueing. Presented with evidence of the faults in his experiments, he retreated somewhat from his original claims, but to the end of his life he persisted in his belief that Hans really did have extraordinary powers of understanding and human-type reasoning. Indeed, the clever horse must have been unusually perceptive and eager to please his trainer to achieve his remarkable performance, even with the help of the unintended signals.

Chimpanzees are much more attentive to their human trainers than most animal species, and consequently the danger of unconscious cueing is especially acute. In fact, it might be suggested that the cueing works both ways. Especially in the case of the studies employing sign language, the interpretation of the signs emitted by the chimpanzee requires a great deal of subjective evaluation on the part of the experimenter. Apes never really produce the gestures of American Sign Language very well but follow the general

---

*Magic is not fashionable by that term. We call it "psychokinesis," "teleportation," "E.S.P.," or other names, by which we mean phenomena that lie outside the mundane world of rational science, physical laws, and verifiable reality. It is a pity that the word *magic* is no longer in vogue, for it is obvious that most of us hunger for a belief in the unbelievable. One should probably not censure those who profit from this hunger. A columnist who claims she can tell your future from the stars is perhaps no less honorable than the actor who tries to make you believe that he is the ghost of the king of Denmark. Both are trying, through their art, to entertain us and to satisfy our longing for the irrational.

patterns of arm movements learned from their trainers. The "seamless movements," as they have been called, of the chimp's arms as he "converses" with his human partner contain embedded in their pattern quite a number of potential meaningful signs. Given that most of the messages reported came immediately after the human experimenter had prompted the animal with the same gestures, it is not surprising that the responses of an animal noted for its natural tendency toward mimicry ("monkey see, monkey do") should contain many of the same "words." Thus not only is the animal given a powerful cue as to what symbols should be appropriate in the exchange, but the experimenter too is cued to look for specific meanings in a somewhat ambiguous movement. Add to this the inherent power of words to combine logically, even when mixed randomly, and we get an impressive number of "hits" in the search for grammatical utterances. I would agree that when the chimpanzee Nim signed "banana me Nim me" he probably was expressing an interest in bananas, and even that he may have expected his action to be rewarded with a long yellow fruit. I would, however, question whether Nim's learned performance is any more convincing as evidence of language acquisition than the behavior of a cat that rubs against your legs in front of the refrigerator door.

The study of language abilities of nonhumans has been far from negative. Ed and Sue Rumbaugh, now at the Yerkes Regional Primate Research Center in Atlanta, have shown great sophistication and inventiveness in eliminating many of the sources of error inherent in the face-to-face interactions between experimenter and subject that are unavoidable in studies using sign language. They rely upon a computer-operated console with lighted symbols controlled by keys that the chimpanzees are trained to press. The computer-controlled symbols make up a vocabulary called "Yerkish." This team has not only shown how well chimpanzees can adapt to an artificial mode of communication, but they have been more meticulous than many experimenters in pointing out the limitations of their animals compared with humans in the development of language skills.

Along with David Premack, Ed and Sue Rumbaugh are outstanding among the various animal experimenters for their ability to go beyond the immediate experiments into the very roots of the relationship between language and intelligence in general. Their many published works about animal intelligence give a much clearer specification of what is meant by human consciousness than appears in most of the psychological literature devoted specifically to the human case. They consider a number of factors, but three seem particularly relevant:

1. *Intentionality.* In this context, *intentionality* means not only wanting the *results* of an exchange, but also showing a deliberate, knowing use of the specific symbol for achieving the desired end. "Knowing" almost begs the question, but the meaning of that term in animal communication studies is limited to what can be studied from the overt behavior and does not imply getting inside the animal's consciousness. Premack provides an ingenious test for whether language is used knowingly by nonhumans.[15] He tried to get his subjects to lie! Lying certainly shows a deliberate manipulation of symbols to produce a willed effect, even when the real facts are contrary to the message. Premack's apes failed the test. They could not lie. (Humans, I regret to add, learn the trick very early. Lying for personal gain is not much different, in essence, from imagining a pig with wings. Both consist of making our symbols assert a condition that does not exist in fact. The immorality of lying is in the motivation of the deception, not in the mere fact of creating a message contrary to reality.)

The Rumbaughs have employed several tests for intentionality. One of the most interesting involved an extensive procedure for eliciting a cooperative use of the computer-displayed artificial symbols by two chimpanzees, Sherman and Austin. The experiments do appear to demonstrate a knowing, as opposed to accidental, use of the correct symbol to communicate between the two animals, but of course they were first trained in the use of the specific symbols, and so it is difficult to know how much of the intentionality can be attributed to the animal and how much to the human experimenter, even when the interaction is between ape and ape, rather than between ape and human.

2. *Accessibility of memory.* Premack makes accessibility an overt criterion for a human-type linguistic capacity. The Rumbaughs say less about it, but they pay considerable attention in their studies to the forgetting and retention of symbols. Ability to perceive synonyms and the ability to recognize relationships between objects not physically present, but indicated by symbols, are tests of the effective use of memory. Apes are not very good at these tasks, and other kinds of evidence strongly suggest a great dependence on training and experimental cues for their retrieval of symbolic vocabulary.

3. *Syntax.* Humans differ basically from all other animals in that we process our symbols syntactically. However impressive the vocabulary a chimpanzee may be trained to recognize and use, no nonhuman has ever been shown to be able to create a sentence. One sees an important difference between the painstaking training of apes to produce a usable vocabulary of a few dozen carefully selected symbols and the joyous, fluent, spontaneous gushing forth of hundreds of words, heard or invented, exhibited hour after hour by a two-year-old human child. But the words are only the bricks, and the real glory of human language is the marvelous ordering of these bricks into towers that stand, buildings of grace and utility—phrases, sentences, paragraphs. A bright two-year-old already shows a comprehension of language structure and an ability to create meanings not just from the use of the symbols themselves, but from their interaction in sentences. His utterances are already so far beyond "gimme tickle gimme" as to make us blush for the poor apes. The syntax, which is so orderly and predictable that every human language can be translated into any other, is at the same time so powerful and complex that no one has ever yet been able to define its elements completely. The system that, as Premack puts it, "grows naturally from the human brain" has defied all efforts to codify its rules, but the rules are

there, and they enable any normal child to outperform all the computers in the world.

Vocabulary without syntax is not language. Bricks are not buildings. Symbols piled together without rules, even when there is intent to communicate, cannot qualify as language, and no experimenter has been able to produce an animal with any sign of comprehension of the larger element of language, its structure. Even the lesser half of language, the use of symbols, has required painstaking training by humans. It does not appear to spring spontaneously to the mind of the developing ape, as it so obviously does to the child.

It seems safe to say that language is a uniquely human accomplishment on this earth. Parrots may talk, and apes may type out commands on a special console, but only when taught to do so by humans. One is reminded of an anecdote about the first synthesis of an organic compound. When Wöhler synthesized urea from inorganic precursors, the vitalist notion that only living things could make organic compounds was put to rest—except for one diehard, who remarked, "Friedrich Wöhler is a living thing!" When computers, parrots, and apes "talk" they do so only as extensions of humans—never as spontaneous, free agents.

Will the apes—or the ants, for that matter—ever make that evolutionary jump that we took so recently? Will our descendants a half-million years from now have linguistic contacts with other animals that are denied to us because we are the first? Predictions are always risky, but since nobody now living will be around to prove me wrong, I will venture to say that it seems most unlikely. Even granting the bare survival of a diversity of species on an increasingly despoiled planet, the peculiar concatenation of circumstances that led to a cross-modal processing ability in the brain of a gregarious, tool-using, big-brained beast is unlikely to recur.

Alternative ways to evolve language might be possible, but once we rule out an adaptationist mechanism, the chances of its happening become negligible, and the problems with the adaptationist paradigm have already been pointed out. Language appeared, not by chance, but through the happy coincidence of a number of developmental and evolutionary trends interacting in an animal for whom a language faculty could provide a powerful selective advantage. Once we had acquired that advantage we wiped out any potential rivals for our linguistic uniqueness, and, alas, we are well on our way to wiping out even the also-rans. Would that recognition of the uniqueness of our common syntax might bring our human race closer together and help us recognize our responsibility to preserve and protect our speechless fellow creatures.

If we cannot hope to converse with other species on earth, what then of our little green men from Arcturus? This question brings us back to the philosophical problem of whether the rules of syntax, and perhaps of logic and of mathematics, are fundamental, unchanging, and the same everywhere. To raise the question is not to suggest that somewhere in the universe there is a world where $2 + 2 = 5$. It asks, rather, whether there might be a world where $2 + 2 = 4$ does not make any sense, and where some other unknown, undreamed-of relationships between what we call numbers do make sense. "Unknown, undreamed-of" does not quite get to the distinction, for I can imagine someone finding a new sort of numerical operation that, when explained, would make perfectly good sense to us, even though we had never thought of it in the past. Suppose, however, that the new relationship was not only unimagined, but so foreign to our way of thinking that it was unimaginable: not just unknown, but, for our minds, unknowable. Let it be so incompatible with the ways we think about numbers that our brains could not hold both kinds of systems. But it could still be valid. An alien but intelligent race could conceivably use its brand of mathematics to build bridges that did not collapse, plot the courses of planets, and count the number of their appendages.

By a similar flight of fancy we might imagine an alien race with a syntax forever untranslatable to our language structures, but workable for them. If we overheard their transmissions with our radio telescopes would we be able to decipher them? Probably not. Would they even be recognizable to us as intelligent messages? Possibly, but there is a reason to suspect that they would look like perfectly random noise in the radio band. Information theory provides an interesting insight into coding mechanisms. If we study the "cost," in numbers of bits, of transmitting a volume of material, we find a curious relationship between the probability of a given message and its information content. The less likely the message, the more information it contains. Warren Weaver called this the "surprisal value" of the information. It fits well with our intuitive ideas about information. If I tell you something you already know, you are not surprised by my message. By the same token, you do not really receive any information from me, whereas if I tell you something really startling and unexpected, it may initiate a very profound reorganization of a lot of your concepts. You have received a lot of information.

Our nervous system makes use of this principle. Sensory receptors economize on their messages by accommodating to a monotonous stimulus. The message sent to the brain might be: "Ho hum, nothing much going on here. Just the same old thing, over and over. I'm going to close down, so you just assume that until you hear otherwise from me, it's just more of the same. 'Bye." When you "tune in" to that sensation, your central sensory areas tell you what is going on, but they do not need to hear directly from the peripheral organ, which has stopped sending. Only when there is a change in the stimulus will a message be sent. The "unexpected" requires information to report. The unsurprising message is very cheap. Announcing "Today is my unbirthday!" is unlikely to get you many presents.

Similarly for a coded language. Samuel F.B. Morse had some understanding of this when he devised his telegraphy code. He used a single dot for e, the most common letter, and longer groups of dots and dashes for the less common characters. Since e comes most often in a typical message, it is the least surprising and therefore ought to require the least amount of information to transmit.

In our horse race example, Joe could save on his message if he used a single bit to transmit the expected information when the favorite horse won, and a longer message when an upset occurred. It is when we reduce our information to a binary code that the curious relationship to randomness emerges. Suppose we translated some message into a binary code consisting of the characters *0* and *1*. What if the message read:

00000000100000000000000000000000000000000000000000000000000000

This is not only boring, it is obviously inefficient. All those *0*'s could have been sent much more cheaply by just saying something like, "The rest is all zeros, until I say stop."

On the other hand, a message like:

011000101000110101010101101110101111100001101010100001111011011000110100

at least requires your attention to get the *0*'s and *1*'s straight. Each "bit" is as unexpected as the last and therefore conveys as much information. By the time you have received 50 *0*'s in succession you are not surprised to find that the 51st bit is also a *0*. The second message contains much more information than the first. What else do we notice about the second message? It looks random. This is a very profound observation. It can be shown rigorously that the more efficient the information coding is, the more random it will look. What we are learning is that there is a fundamental relationship between entropy and information. Entropy can be defined as the degree of randomness in a system. The greater the entropy, the greater the amount of information required to describe the system. In some sense, a perfectly random system has no information at all, but in the sense we are interested in, it would take vastly more information to specify the location and motion of every molecule of gas in a random, high entropy state than in a case where all the molecules were rigidly bound together in one small volume.

This discovery about the nature of information is by no means trivial. Since we already have a powerful body of knowledge about thermodynamics, the relationship between information and entropy provides us with some very useful tools for uncovering additional relationships. For example, there is a formal mathematical relationship between entropy and energy. Therefore we can deduce that information, too, is convertible into energy, or, more usefully, energy into information. Thus it is no accident that we speak of "cost" and "cheapness" when discussing information. We are accustomed to thinking of energy as being costly, so when we recognize the similarities between energy and information, we can better understand why biological systems have needed to evolve efficient methods for information processing.

Our hypothetical intelligent civilization that is transmitting messages will presumably be at least as smart as we are about these matters and will have devised a code that is efficient. That means that the messages will look as random as noise. We may never recognize the message, even if we do intercept it. We may have already received many of them.

And so, if these arguments are valid, we are truly alone in the universe. Our linguistic uniqueness, which makes consciousness possible, also sets us apart from all other creatures, here as elsewhere, now and evermore.

How should we deal with this knowledge?

Human culture has always been concerned with the problem. Man has never been humble about his position in the world or the universe. Even the gods of his myths have always had human affairs as their chief concern. Earth was the center, Heaven was close, all the rest of creation was subservient to human domination. But now, science has undermined the basis for our pride. Step by step we have been dethroned. Our earth is a minor planet of a mediocre star in a suburban branch of a typical galaxy. Many find it hard to believe that God molded us in His hands and breathed life into our bodies "made in His image." Rather, it was left to the slow and risky processes of random mutation and selection to raise us from the common lot of all the other beasts. Human culture, which ought to be our proudest achievement, is found by some to be a ruthless monster, grinding the poor to dust, exploiting the weak, and finally spawning a technology that is despoiling the earth itself until we are faced with the dismal choice of atomic annihilation or choking in our own pollution.

The progressive dethronement of mankind by Copernicus, Darwin, and Marx was completed by Freud. If we believe him, we find that we are no longer the lords even of our own minds, but helpless victims of too-rigorous toilet training, suppressed sexual drives, and archaic credos.

The message of this chapter is that we cannot look to any other source for help. We are the best that the earth could produce. There will never be another chance, for the evolutionary die is cast for all other brainy species, committing them to a path that is unlikely to lead to a conscious intelligence. Likewise, there is little hope from beyond the stars. If other intelligent life exists within reach, it is overwhelmingly unlikely to be of a sort that could even communicate with us, let alone identify with our special needs. Even God no longer seems to intervene. If He still speaks from a burning bush, we do not listen, nor even bother to stone His prophets; we are more likely to shut them up in custodial institutions or at best ignore them.

So we are left with no one but ourselves. We are indeed the custodians, not only of our own fate, but of the whole world. Indeed, of the universe. Our task is to learn to know ourselves. We cannot deny our culture, but we can strive to use it better—to preserve the world rather than despoil it, and to improve the lives of all people, not just the few. If we cannot hope to truly communicate with our brother animal species, we can cherish them and protect them.

This is a hard message, but we have the most potent asset the world has ever produced—our conscious minds. The capacity of the human brain is unimaginably greater than we have guessed. We do not need to wait for some hoped-for evolutionary increase in size and ability. It is already there, waiting to be used. Likewise, human culture provides an almost limitless potential for development. It is both the product and the tool of our intellect. The exponential expansion of our knowledge feeds an ever-increasing power to use our minds better. We are so critical of our failures that we overlook the multitude of problems we have solved. It is our successes that have increased our expectations to a point where we are sensitive to problems which a cruder age ignored.

Perhaps our salvation lies in the recognition of the incredible potential of the human mind. The human species has studied itself throughout its history. Generations of philosophers, anatomists, psychologists, and physiologists have made their contributions, but we are only now beginning to comprehend the majesty of that gray lump in our heads. Napoleon once attributed his military success to "a will to win." In this age of indecision we have too often been overwhelmed by the magnitude of our problems, and perhaps too humble about our power to overcome them.

If we must stand alone in the universe as conscious beings, we should take pride in that fact. If we feel humble about what our intellects have produced so far, at least we should recognize that we are the best there is. Fifty thousand years is not a very long time when you consider that the dinosaurs had a hundred and sixty million. We have come a long way from Neanderthal. Let us hope that the journey is only beginning.

References

1. A. A. Milne, "In the Fashion," from *When We Were Very Young* (New York: E. P. Dutton & Co., Inc., 1924).

2. Jan Jelinek, "European *Homo erectus* and the Origin of Homo sapiens," in *Current Argument on Early Man*, ed. Lars-Konig Konigsson (Oxford: Pergamon Press, 1980).

3. G. Sacher, "Maturation and Longevity in Relation to Cranial Capacity in Hominid Evolution," in *Primate Functional Morphology and Evolution*, ed. R. Tuttle (Paris: Mouton, 1975), p. 417.

4. Stephen Jay Gould and R. C. Lewontin, "The Spandrels of San Marco and the Panglossian Paradigm," *Proceedings of the Royal Society of London*, B205 (1979), 582.

5. David Premack, "Language and Intelligence in Ape and Man," *American Scientist*, 64 (November 1976), 674.

6. T. S. Eliot, "The Dry Salvages," from *Four Quartets* (New York: Harcourt, Brace and Co., 1950). From "The Dry Salvages" in *Four Quartets*, copyright 1943 by T. S. Eliot; renewed 1971 by Esme Valerie Eliot. Reprinted by permission of Harcourt Brace Jovanovich, Inc.

7. Richard Dawkins, *The Selfish Gene* (New York: Oxford University Press, 1976).

8. Norman Geschwind, "The Anatomical Basis of Hemi-

spheric Differentiation," in *Hemisphere Function in the Human Brain*, ed. S. J. Dimond and J. G. Beaumont (New York: Wiley, 1974), pp. 7–24.

9. Miguel de Unamuno, *The Tragic Sense of Life in Men and Nations* (Princeton: Princeton University Press, 1972), p. 5.

10. M. S. Gazzaniga, "The Split Brain in Man," *Scientific American*, 217 (August 1967), 24.

11. Emily Dickinson, "The brain is wider than the sky," *The Complete Poems of Emily Dickinson*, ed. Thomas H. Johnson (Boston: Little, Brown and Co., 1960). Reprinted by permission of the publishers and the Trustees of Amherst College from *The Poems of Emily Dickinson*, edited by Thomas H. Johnson, Cambridge, Mass.: The Belknap Press of Harvard University Press, Copyright 1951,© 1955, 1979, 1983 by the President and Fellows of Harvard College.

12. E. Roy John, "Switchboard versus Statistical Theories of Learning and Memory," *Science*, 177 (8 September 1972), 850–64.

13. William Wordsworth, "Lines composed a few miles above Tintern Abbey."

14. C. E. Shannon and Warren Weaver, *Mathematical Theory of Communications* (Urbana: University of Illinois Press, 1949).

15. David Premack, "Language and Intelligence in Ape and Man," *American Scientist*, 64 (November 1976), 682.

16. W. H. Auden, "Their Lonely Betters," in *Collected Shorter Poems 1927–1957* (London: Faber and Faber Ltd., 1966). Copyright 1951 by W. H. Auden. Reprinted from *W. H. Auden: Collected Poems*, edited by Edward Mendelson, by permission of Random House, Inc.

17. Richard Adams, *Watership Down* (Baltimore: Penguin Books, Inc., 1974).

Glossary

Adaptationist: One who espouses the theory that every biological structure was evolved by the principle of selection for fitness.

Anthropoid: Literally, "man-like"; refers to the tailless primates but is usually applied to the great apes—the gorillas and the chimpanzees.

Axon: The nerve fiber carrying nerve impulses away from the cell body, as opposed to the dendrite, which carries impulses toward the cell body.

Bilateral specialization: The differentiation of the right and left halves of an organism to perform different functions. Used specifically of the brain, where specialization has led to the dominance of the right hand in most humans and the localization of certain mental functions, such as language, on one side or the other of the cerebrum.

Bipedal: Having two legs rather than four. Quadrupeds (four-legged animals) are more common among the terrestrial vertebrates. Birds and hominids are the major living bipeds.

BIT: Binary digIT, a single unit in a binary number system. Since there can be no simpler system capable of conveying information, the BIT is the smallest possible unit of information, and therefore the number of bits is a measure of the information content of a message.

Cochlea: The sense organ of hearing among the higher vertebrates. It is a snail-shaped tube located in the inner ear, containing the "hair cells" which convert sound vibrations into nerve impulses with a pattern conveying coded information about the amplitude and frequency of the sound stimulus.

Deterministic: A term applied to a system that follows a knowable pattern so that the outcome of any event can, at least in principle, be predicted. Newtonian mechanics is deterministic; quantum mechanics deals with nondeterministic events. The precise location of an electron is indeterminate.

Endocast: A cast made of the inside of a cavity. Skulls sometimes fill up with mud that eventually turns to stone, thus preserving a fossil record of the contours of the brain, even if the skull itself is lost or eroded.

Entropy: The measure of the degree of randomness or disorder in a system. Entropy is related to information, both mathematically and intuitively.

Epicritic: A sensory experience in which the location of the stimulus is a part of the perception; as contrasted to *protopathic*, the term applied to a sensation that is not specifically localized to any part of the body.

Epithelium: A tissue that covers an organ or lines a cavity in an animal—for example, the outer layer of skin or the lining of a blood vessel.

Exaptation: A more appropriate word to substitute for the term *preadaptation*. Exaptation is a change in the function of some evolved structure or mechanism to meet a biological need for which it was not specifically evolved.

Femur: The thigh bone, usually the longest bone in the body of a land animal.

Gracile: Having a small-boned, delicate build; a light frame.

Hominid: Any of the man-like creatures belonging to the family *Hominidae*, which includes the genus *Homo* and a number of extinct genera.

Laser: A device that generates coherent light—that is, light in which all of the waves are exactly in phase with one another.

Limbic system: A loosely connected set of structures within the brain that forms a kind of margin or "limb" surrounding the thalamus. Collectively these structures are concerned with the emotions; thus *limbic system* is sometimes used as a synonym for the affective brain.

Morphology: Form or structure. Also the study of structure, whether at the level of the whole body, organs, cells, or subcellular objects.

Neolithic: Pertaining to the New Stone Age—a period of high culture and technology but preceding the discovery of smelting and the use of metals. American Indians were essentially a Neolithic culture at the time of the European arrival in the New World.

Neurotransmitter: A chemical substance released by the endings of one neuron that causes an immediate reaction on the adjacent neuron, resulting in the transmission, blocking, or otherwise modifying of a nerve impulse.

Nucleus: In neuroanatomy a nucleus is not a structure inside a cell, but rather a collection of neurons forming a patch of gray matter located inside a surrounding mass of white matter within the central nervous system.

Occipital lobe: The hindmost portion of the cerebrum, consisting mostly of the visual processing region of the sensory brain.

Ontogeny: The developmental or embryonic history of a specific individual.

Phylogeny: The evolutionary history of a species.

Preadaptation: A theoretical concept describing an evolutionary change that prepares an organism for some need but that arose as a consequence of selection for some unrelated function.

Primates: The order consisting of all living and extinct apes, monkeys, and hominids.

Robust: Large-boned, as opposed to gracile. A draft horse is robust; a race horse is gracile.

Simian: The higher primates, including Old World monkeys, New World monkeys, and the anthropoids. *Prosimian* refers to both the evolutionary predecessors of the simians and also the "lower" primates, including lemurs, tarsiers, and lorises.

Statistical: A term applied to a system, such as a complex neural network, in which the outcome of a rational sequence is lawful and predictable, although the individual steps of the process are neither localizable nor knowable with certainty.

Sympatric: A term describing populations of closely related organisms occupying the same territory at the same time. Such populations are unlikely to evolve into separate species because their members will probably interbreed.

Taxonomy: The science of classification of organisms. Modern taxonomy is based on the systems developed by Linnaeus.

Suggested Readings

Bronowski, Jacob, *The Origins of Knowledge and Imagination* (New Haven: Yale University Press, 1978).

Dobzhansky, Theodosius, *Mankind Evolving: The Evolution of the Human Species* (New Haven: Yale University Press, 1967).

Eccles, John C., *The Understanding of the Brain* (New York: McGraw-Hill Book Co., 1977).

Dimond, Stuart J., and David A. Blizard (eds.), *Evolution and Lateralization of the Brain*, Annals, Vol. 299 (New York: The New York Academy of Sciences, 1977).

Gould, Stephen Jay, *Ever Since Darwin: Reflections on Natural History* (New York: Norton, 1977).

Harnad, Stevan R., Horst D. Steklis, and Jane Lancaster (eds.), *Origins and Evolution of Language and Speech*, Annals, Vol. 280 (New York: The New York Academy of Sciences, 1976).

Hill, W. C. Osman, *Evolutionary Biology of the Primates* (London: Academic Press, 1972).

Johanson, Donald, and Maitland Edey, *Lucy: The Beginnings of Humankind* (New York: Warner Books, 1981).

SUGGESTED READINGS

Le Gros Clark, W. E., *History of the Primates: An Introduction to the Study of Fossil Man* (Chicago: University of Chicago Press, 1957).

Oakley, Kenneth P., *Man the Tool-Maker* (London: Trustees of the British Museum, 1975).

Pfeiffer, John E., *The Emergence of Man* (New York: Harper & Row, 1972).

Sagan, Carl, *The Dragons of Eden: Speculations on the Evolution of Human Intelligence* (New York: Random House, 1977).

Sarnat, Harvey B., and Martin G. Netsky, *Evolution of the Nervous System* (New York: Oxford University Press, 1974).

Solecki, Ralph S., *Shanidar, the First Flower People* (New York: Alfred A. Knopf, Inc., 1971).

Szalay, Frederick S., and Eric Delson, *Evolutionary History of the Primates* (New York: Academic Press, 1979).

Watson, William, *Flint Implements* (London: Trustees of the British Museum, 1975).

Index

INDEX

INDEX

INDEX